# POWER ON ICE

# POWER ON ICE

Denis Potvin

with Stan Fischler

HARPER & ROW, PUBLISHERS

New York   Hagerstown

San Francisco   London

To Debbie, my parents, my brother,
and all the coaches who have helped me
throughout my career

POWER ON ICE. Copyright © 1977 by Denis Potvin, Ltd. and Stan Fischler. All rights reserved. Printed in the United States of America. No part of this book may be used or reproduced in any manner whatsoever without written permission except in the case of brief quotations embodied in critical articles and reviews. For information address Harper & Row, Publishers, Inc., 10 East 53rd Street, New York, N.Y. 10022. Published simultaneously in Canada by Fitzhenry & Whiteside Limited, Toronto.

Library of Congress Cataloging in Publication Data
Potvin, Denis.
    Power on ice.

    1. Hockey—United States. 2. Potvin, Denis.
I. Fischler, Stan, joint author. II. Title.
GV848.4.U6P67   1977    796.9′62′0973      76–9198
ISBN 0–06–013387–2

FIRST EDITION

Designed by C. Linda Dingler

77 78 79 80  10 9 8 7 6 5 4 3 2 1

# CONTENTS

*A section of photographs follows page 92.*

# ACKNOWLEDGMENTS

The authors wish to thank the following people, without whom the book could not have been accomplished: Tony Andrea, Edd Griles, Harriet Cook, and the rest of the good people at People & Properties; also Ray Volpe, Rhoda Dreifus, Debbie Potvin, Jon Trontz, Ira Lacher, Shirley Fischler, Dave Rubenstein, Richard Friedman, David Cogan, Karen Robertson, Jack Goldstein, Joe Pagnotta, Clem Finkenstaedt and Terry Foley.

Exceptional thanks are in order for Joe Resnick, Associate Editor of *Action Sports Hockey,* who provided expert help, above and beyond the call of duty, in transcribing the Potvin tapes—expeditiously, accurately, and without a single word of complaint. If Resnick were in the NHL, he'd win the Hart Trophy.

Finally, the guidance, inspiration, and general patience offered by our editor, one of the genuinely nice people (in the very best sense of the word) in the business, Joe Vergara, deserves our additional thanks.

# FOREWORD

If a Las Vegas oddsmaker were making book on the chances of one S. I. Fischler collaborating with Denis Potvin on a book, he probably would conservatively rate it as a 1,000-to-1 possibility. On the one hand, there was the reporter from Brooklyn with a reputation for being critical and who proved the point by withering the New York Islanders in their first, fumbling year in the National Hockey League. On the other hand, there was the French-Canadian hockey player from Ottawa who, at one point, was a target of the critic's fire.

How, then, did they ever manage to meet—let alone produce this insightful look at the world of hockey, business, and, of course, the Islanders?

For starters, they did get to meet each other, and a mutual respect developed immediately. It all happened thanks to a shared friend, writer Jon Trontz, whom the editor and the athlete had known since Potvin became an Islander.

At the time, I had just begun to do the "color" commentary of Islanders' home games for Home Box Office, the cable television network. It was my job to find between-periods guests and, one night, I decided that Denis would be appropriate since he was disabled by an injury to his leg and, therefore, would not be in uniform.

I was acutely aware, however, that Potvin, like many other players, might have taken a dim view of some of my harsher columns in *The Sporting News* and might, quite justifiably, refuse to appear on television with me. I asked my friend, Jon Trontz, whether he thought Denis would appear.

"I'll ask him," said Jon, "and knowing what a class guy Denis is, I have a feeling that he'll show up."

Frankly, I had my doubts. After all, Potvin had the perfect alibis; not only had I been critical, but he was *hors de combat*. He was using a pair of crutches to move around and certainly would have a difficult time reaching the TV area.

In a matter of minutes, Trontz returned with the news. Denis would be delighted to appear. And, sure enough, between the first and second periods Potvin showed up (two ushers were required to lift him over the protective metal bars that surround the TV area) and was the sparkling, witty interview he always is. More than that, we both discovered that we had something in common—an interest in things other than hockey.

About a half-year later we had dinner together and discussed the idea of Denis' doing a book. We met with Joe Vergara, my thoughtful editor at Harper & Row, and agreed that Potvin had enough to say about hockey—and life—to make such a project worthwhile. Yet even after we had signed our contracts and begun work on the book I suffered doubts.

Would Denis, a French-Canadian, have sufficient mastery over English to deliver his points accurately? Would he have enough time, during the heat of the homestretch (when we met regularly for taping sessions) to work on the book? How would his charming wife, Debbie, affect the project?

The questions themselves suggested that the project would not be an easy one. But Denis being Denis, all the negatives were turned to positives. Not only was his English impeccable, it was more polished than mine. Although time was a problem, Potvin *made* time, much more so than athletes with whom I had previously collaborated. And Debbie was a marvelous and beautiful catalyst to the development of the book.

During the course of our collaboration I came to know Denis as a friend as much as an athlete. He astonished me with his grasp of the world around him and his genuine, insatiable interest in everything, from the arts to the subway system of New York City.

He is a marvelous, Renaissance man, and the opportunity to work with him and to get to know him goes down as one of the most gratifying experiences of my career.

STAN FISCHLER

*New York City*
*July 1976*

# POWER ON ICE

# 1

## "DENIS, YOU ARE THE BEST!"

"Denis, I have some very important news for you," said the voice from the 79th floor of the Empire State Building.

It was late morning and I was feeling perfectly punko, sitting in my Garden City apartment. I had just finished poring over my bank account and discovered I had $500 left in the bank. Unfortunately, I had to write checks amounting to $1,500.

In the next minute, the voice at the other end of the line converted my depression into modified joy. It was David Cogan, my personal representative, accountant, and browbeater. Cogan, who sometimes reminds me of a cross between Edward G. Robinson and Jimmy Cagney, has the deepest furrowed brows I've ever seen, but this time I knew he was smiling. I could tell by the laugh in his voice.

"Denis, you are the best. I have just been informed that you've won the Norris Trophy. You've replaced Bobby Orr. You are Numero Uno."

Winning the Norris Trophy—who could believe it? It had been my dream since I was old enough to walk. But everyone knew that Bobby Orr owned the prize; he had won it every single season since 1968. Now it was mine.

"How do you feel?" asked Cogan, who had just negotiated a five-year contract for me that boggled my mind. There was a moment of silence.

"Right now, David, I've got no feeling, just a large lump in my throat!"

It was in many ways the biggest moment of my life. In three years I had accomplished everything I had set out to do, and then some. I wanted to win the National Hockey League's rookie-of-the-year award, and I did. I wanted to make the NHL's First All-Star Team, and I did. More than anything, I wanted to take the Norris Trophy away from Orr, and now it was done.

But did I really deserve it? Orr had been out of action for most of the 1975–76 season and Brad Park had suffered a bum start with the Rangers before he was dealt to Boston.

I put the bankbook down, thanked Cogan for calling, and excused myself. I wanted an hour alone to digest all that had happened to me—someone who had not yet reached the age of 23. I walked outside and strolled down Franklin Street. The more I walked, the happier I felt.

"Denis," I muttered to myself, "you didn't win this thing because of your good looks."

I stared at people coming out of the shops, and they all seemed to be smiling, as if they knew I had just won the Norris and wanted to share in my happiness. By now I was nearly skipping down the street like a delirious little kid. Then I slowed down and the vignettes of victory came to mind.

My team, the New York Islanders, had been the team of destiny in the spring of 1975. We were only three years old at the time but we had beaten the 49-year-old New York Rangers in the opening round of the Stanley Cup playoffs. Then we came from behind, 0 games to 3, and beat the eight-year-old Pittsburgh Penguins. And *then,* again down 0 games to 3, we won three straight from the Stanley Cup–champion Philadelphia Flyers.

What we had done was *more* than a miracle. It was a super-phenomenon, even better than the New York Mets winning their first World Series. But, as they say on Madison Avenue and on the Long Island Expressway, that was old business.

When September 1975 arrived, the question hockey fans wanted answered was how real—how phony—was the Islanders' miracle? The answer came in April 1976. We beat the Rangers out of a playoff berth. We had the best power play and the best penalty-killers in the NHL and we insisted upon making still *more* miracles.

How, you ask, do you make a miracle?

In 1976 our first playoff opponents were the Vancouver Canucks, a strong team filled with six-footers. During the regular season the Canucks had killed us with three wins, two ties, and *no* losses. Besides, we finished the schedule flatter than a hockey puck while the Canucks were hot. Our best sharpshooters had lost their touch. "What are you going to do for us now?" demanded veteran New York *Daily News* hockey writer Gene Ward.

We opened the game shakier than an operator of a pneumatic drill.

Our ace goalie, Glenn "Chico" Resch, fanned on a couple of easy shots and the cynics figured we'd lost the best-of-three series in two straight.

"This team bends," said our wise, portly manager Bill Torrey between the first and second periods, "but we don't break."

We rebounded to beat Vancouver, 5–3, and then we flew to British Columbia, where we knocked off the Canucks in two straight games, with a 3–1 decision. Now, could we make a second miracle?

Everybody thought we'd need one when it turned out that our second-round opponents would be the Buffalo Sabres, last year's Stanley Cup finalists (they missed the Cup by only one game!) and a team that had murdered us all year. What chance did we have against a team bristling with such big guns as Richard Martin, Gil Perreault, and René Robert of the famed and feared "French Connection"?

Obviously, no chance.

At least it looked that way after the first two games in Buffalo. We were bombed, 5–3, in the opener and then lost, 3–2, a heartbreaking sudden-death overtime game. The scene shifted to our home rink, Nassau Coliseum.

The Sabres had openly proclaimed they could beat us with their "Stop Denis Potvin" movement. I was flattered. They tried to crowd and hound my every turn, and they succeeded because I was too stationary in the first two games. I was trying to move the puck instead of moving up myself. They were getting close to me and closing the lanes. I knew I had to move more and take chances.

To bounce back and make the second miracle, we knew that we had to play Buffalo head-on and forget about sparring with them, matching lines, and worrying about the little things. Still, our most fervent supporters doubted that we would win a game, let alone the series, from Buffalo.

CAN ISLANDERS REBOUND? shouted a headline in *The New York Post* on April 15, 1976, on the afternoon of the third game of the series. The suggestion was that we couldn't. Our captain, Eddie Westfall, had a serious foot injury. Forwards Jude Drouin, André St. Laurent, and Bob Nystrom had been stretched out in the trainer's room with an assortment of wounds that would seriously hamper their play. Still, Bill Torrey wasn't worried, nor was our bespectacled and always calm coach, Al Arbour.

"We've lost two," said Torrey, "but we still showed a lot of guts. Certain guys are hurt physically, but I can't complain about their heart."

In the next hours we made Torrey's words look good. Our team came back home and put body—and mouth—to the Sabres and beat them. We played *our* game, forechecking like a horde of leeches on skates. Some of our guys began to talk about how the Buffalo players could be intimidated by heavy body work.

But we also knew that one win meant nothing. The second game at Nassau would be the decisive one. If we could take that, we could go the route against Buffalo.

I had a good feeling in my head and legs as we trooped from our dressing room at the Coliseum out over the rubber matting to the ice, where the arena was already half-filled with fans. It was Saturday night, April 17, 1976, and I thought to myself, there's no way we're going to lose if I play my aggressive game. During the warm-up, I did some self-hypnosis while we peppered our goalies Glenn Resch and Billy Smith with shots. "Remember, Denis," I said to myself, "no daydreaming tonight!"

Daydreaming is always a problem. Sure, I'm a hockey player and I'm *supposed* to concentrate on hockey 25 hours a day; at least that's the fantasy a lot of fans have. But I'm more than a hockey player. I'm a businessman. I'm part owner of a Manhattan corporation called People & Properties. I'm an art collector. I devour books like they're cotton candy. There is more to Denis Potvin than meets the ice and, sometimes, I find myself thinking about Picasso at the Museum of Modern Art rather than the puck at the Coliseum.

Not, however, on this night. The referee dropped the puck for the opening face-off and instantly the Sabres tried to refute the whispers that they were "chicken." Their big captain, Jim Schoenfeld, began throwing his weight around—and, within 19 seconds, was thrown into the penalty box for two minutes. It was time for our power play, once the laughing stock of the NHL but now so vaunted it put the fear of God in enemy goaltenders.

Coach Al Arbour sent me out on the ice with our "Kid Line" of Bryan Trottier, Clark Gillies, and Billy Harris. My older brother, Jean, completed the high-scoring unit. The man we wanted to beat was Sabres goalie Gerry Desjardins, a pudgy veteran who had been with the Islanders in my rookie year.

Oh! How I wanted to pump that six-ounce hunk of vulcanized rubber past that mask of his. With 11 seconds remaining on our power play, I finally got my chance. Trottier was controlling the puck in the Sabres' zone, his face totally impassive as usual, holding the puck, holding, holding, waiting for a Buffalo defender to commit himself foolishly.

His patience paid off; a defenseman rushed for Bryan, leaving an opening near Desjardins. I sensed it the way a shark smells blood and skated like hell for the left face-off circle. Trottier skimmed me the kind of pass that can only be described as smoother than a soft B flat on a slide trombone.

On this play Desjardins moved to the left side of the net, hunching his 30 pounds of gear and pads together, waiting for my strike like the mongoose counters the cobra. I came straight in on the left, nabbed the puck at the face-off circle, and whipped it past Desjardins before he could blink his eyes.

The Sabres were not quite ready to play dead. René Robert tied the score less than four minutes later. Strike one. We had to counterattack, but that's often easier said (in the dressing room *after* the game) than done.

It wasn't until the 13-minute mark of the second period that we found a crack in the Sabres' armor. Desjardins blocked a shot by my pal, road roommate, and defense partner, Gerry Hart. But the goalie foolishly fell to the ice trying to cover up the puck, causing his defenseman Lee Fogolin to tumble into him across the goal mouth. The puck conveniently squirted loose, and Garry Howatt, the only epileptic in big-league hockey and one of the most courageous and toughest men alive, put it home.

It was 2–1 for us and now it was a question whether we could seize the momentum and stifle Buffalo's will to win.

Wouldn't it be nice if I could personally salt this game away with one more blast? A few minutes later, I got my chance. The Sabres were reeling, having killed another of our power plays, and our captain Eddie Westfall, licensed airplane pilot, wit, and total inspiration, found the puck at his feet inside the Sabres' territory. He deflected it to me with his skate and I burst in on my antagonist, Desjardins.

A goaltender has an option when abandoned by his defense and confronted one-on-one by the enemy. He can remain in his crease and hope to make a last-second move in the direction of the shot; or he can challenge the shooter to make the first move and hope that he will rush the foe into an impulsive mistake.

Desjardins moved his hulk at me. "You've got a little time," I thought to myself, "so take a good look, Denis. See what Gerry has to give you."

I looked hard enough in that brief moment to discover a bit of air on the short side. Desjardins was probably trying to lure me to fire at the long side, hoping to cover up in time. I wasn't going to fall for his lure; I gambled on the short side and that's where I put it.

Strike Three on Desjardins.

Billy Harris scored another goal for us, and we eventually skated off to a thunderous roar with a 4–2 triumph. But we still hadn't won a playoff game at Buffalo's Auditorium, and that would not be easy. The Aud, as they call it, is a smaller than standard size rink. Nearly every NHL ice surface measures 85 feet wide by 200 feet long, but the old Aud is only 196 feet long, which makes it easier to handle for a team such as the Sabres that plays there all the time.

I couldn't believe the excitement when we landed in Buffalo. *The Buffalo Evening News* carried a big spread about fans staying up all night outside The Aud to buy tickets. A photo showed kids standing in the all-night vigil; next to that was a story by Dick Johnston, headlined DECEPTIVE DENIS KEYS N.Y.

To my surprise, Desjardins had some kind words to say about me. He conceded that I was "the most dangerous" of the Islanders.

"They try to get the puck to him," added defenseman Bill Hajt. "He's got the good shot; both a wrist and a slap shot."

Desjardins allowed that he knew a bit about my shot. "Denis' shot is deceptive," the goalie explained. "He uses a wrist shot more than he does the slap shot. He plays like Bobby Orr and Brad Park—pass the puck and go, take a return pass."

I thought to myself, "How sweet it would be if I could get free for some of that in Game Five."

Patience was my virtue this time. Buffalo gave us quite a going over for two and a half periods and as the clock ticked past the 15-minute mark of the third period we were down, 2–3. We desperately needed a break, and it finally came when J. P. Parise—the man we call "Jeep," whose beard is so thick he looks like he needs a shave ten seconds after shaving—delivered a pass to me in the slot and I made just the kind of shot Desjardins had been telling the press about a day earlier.

I had tied the score and now it was time for sudden-death overtime: the first goal wins the game. Or so we thought. There was 19 seconds remaining in the period when a face-off was held deep in Buffalo ice.

Westfall won the draw and kicked the puck to André St. Laurent, who skated with it behind the Sabres' goal. Standing at the blue line was one of the nicest guys in the world and one of the best defensive defensemen, Bert Marshall.

Unfortunately, Marshall's shot is so weak we kid him that it's more like a pass. St. Laurent looked to Bert and sent the pass to him. When Bert gets a pass like that, we don't expect him to do much; maybe pass off and hope somebody else scores. Bert, you see, had not scored a goal *all season.*

I was on the ice watching the move. Bert wound up and *didn't* pass. He shot at the mass in front of Desjardins. I don't know how long I sat there looking, but I was in awe. The puck disappeared. The red light went on and the whole team jumped over the boards and smothered our buddy.

Bert was giggling and laughing and kept saying, "I don't believe it. My God, I don't believe it!"

Minutes later we were in the dressing room, climbing all over each other with joy. Days later we had pulled off another miracle by knocking Buffalo out of the playoffs. And only a month later I was voted the Norris Trophy and First NHL All-Star. (Shortly after that I learned that I was picked as a starting defenseman for Team Canada 1976 to play in the Canada Cup tournament.)

Now *I* was saying, "I don't believe it!"

Neither did Armand Potvin, for whom I had won it as much as for anyone else. If it weren't for my dad, who had nearly been in the NHL himself, it never would have happened. He made me a hockey player.

# 2

# LEARNING TO SKATE

Hull, Quebec, just across the river from Ottawa, Ontario, the capital of Canada, was my birthplace and Hull-Ottawa remained my home from childhood until the last year I played junior hockey, when I moved up to the NHL.

Hockey was in my blood right from the start, which is the way my father wanted it. Dad had been a pretty good player himself, and he might have made it all the way to the NHL were it not for an injury. He played junior hockey for a team in Perth, Ontario, which was, at the time, a highly respected club in Canada.

This was just before the start of World War II, when junior hockey had reached a very competitive level in Canada. Dad's team skated against some of the best, including the Verdun (Quebec) Maple Leafs, a Montreal-based club. The star of the Maple Leafs was none other than Maurice "The Rocket" Richard, one of the greatest scorers in hockey history.

Eventually, Dad made it up to the NHL—or at least an NHL training camp. He was invited by the Detroit Red Wings to try out for the big club and, who knows, he might have made it. But bad luck intervened: In training camp with the Wings he suffered a broken back so serious that it not only ended Dad's hockey career then and there but also prevented him from serving in the Canadian armed forces during World War II. The injury still troubles him to this day.

I'm sure Dad's misfortune played a part in his directing his sons toward a hockey career. There were three of us: Bob the oldest, Jean, and Denis. We were the branches of the Potvin hockey tree; Dad was the trunk, the original from which we kids grew.

Like any normal son, I was curious about my father's job, how much money he made, what his office looked like, and who his colleagues were, and I tried to pump him for information. Ottawa is to Canada what Washington, D.C., is to the United States. It's a government town, and many of the people who live there are burdened with bureaucratic desk jobs that bore them to tears. My father was one of them. He worked for the Department of Supply and Services; he was an administrator in a placement office. But Dad would never discuss his work at home if he could help it. I'm sure that was because he didn't enjoy it. His heart was in sports and it was a permanent blow to him to know that a potentially bright NHL career had been wiped out by a broken back.

That simply magnified his dislike for his job. It was something he had to do, so he got up five days a week and did it! I could sense his feeling of despair, and from that I developed the feeling that I never ever wanted to fall into a similar rut. Even before I knew that I'd make a career of hockey, I felt I never wanted to fall into a job I hated. He had a boring, repetitive life. Denis, I told myself, never let that happen to you.

And even though Dad never told me how much money he made, he didn't have to, because I found out in other ways.

Dad took his original skates from junior hockey and passed them on to Bob. When they were too small for Bob, he gave them to Jean, and, eventually, they came to me. I learned how to play the game on a fourth-generation pair of skates. By this time these skates weren't in the best of shape, and they were very poorly insulated against the cold (which we had plenty of in Ottawa). To keep my feet warm in those ancient skates I'd sprinkle a lot of pepper inside the boot before I went out to play. That would last for hours, and it always worked.

To get ready for a hockey game, I'd go down to the basement, open up the big equipment box, and dig through to find my brothers' old stuff—a shin pad, then another (that didn't match), a maroon pair of hockey pants held together in the back by black tape, and other ancient odds and ends. I knew it had to be that way because Dad couldn't afford new equipment. And I never asked for anything other than what was in that big box.

Every December I'd go downtown and ogle a lot of toys in the department store windows, but I never got the toys I wanted, and I accepted that as a fact of life. Then, one Christmas, a shiny new pair of Black Panther ice skates showed up under the Christmas tree, and I suddenly became the happiest kid in all Canada.

You see, everything in our lives in those days was geared around hockey, from early fall to the first thaw of spring. At the age of three I learned how to skate in the backyard behind our house. Mom and Dad would lay out the rink, flood it when the temperature fell below freezing, and shovel off the snow after a storm. They didn't have to push me very much because in our family there was a built-in competition between Bob, Jean, and myself that was especially great for me as the youngest Potvin.

Jean is four years older than I, which meant that at the time I was learning to play hockey he was one of "the big guys," though still young enough to be within my range. I wasn't timid about demanding his time or insisting that I be allowed to play with his gang. In retrospect, I'd say I was pretty precocious. But I was already rather big for my age (I'm now a 204-pound six-footer), and I felt a very strong inner push to become better and to play with the better athletes.

This turned out to be the pattern of my entire playing career right up to the NHL; I was always skating with the older fellows, the better players. When I started in junior hockey, I was only 14 years old and skating against big guys who were 19 and 20. None of this would have been possible if Jean hadn't been very tolerant of his kid brother and, more important, very understanding.

But I found that Lucille Potvin, my mom, was always the one I'd turn to for comfort. She was a strong woman, yet I was never afraid of her. In our house there was a clear demarcation of roles. Dad was the breadwinner while Mom ran the house—right down to buying the clothes for me, Jean, *and* my father. It was a typical French-Canadian family in that sense.

Like Dad, Mom brought a very definite inner strength to Jean and me. If we were in the country, for instance, and picked up a snake or played with spiders, she'd never betray any fear. Always, there was that reassuring cool about her. And if I got hurt, she'd say, "Denis, it's not the first time you've been bruised and it won't be the last. You're a big boy and, just remember, it's going to heal."

There was plenty of love and emotion in our family but very little pity. That, more than anything, conditioned Jean and me against the pain we would inevitably suffer in pro hockey.

Mom was also a big help to me because she never discouraged my interest in hockey from Day One of my first scrimmage behind the house. So, you see, I had a tremendous amount of motivation behind me, with still another "hidden" source of energy coming from distant Montreal. This catalyst was a man named René Lecavalier.

Lecavalier is neither player, coach, nor manager. He is the French-language broadcaster for the Canadian Broadcasting System and the man known as "The Voice of the Montreal Canadiens." Even before I learned to read and write I was listening to René Lecavalier. Since we spoke only French in our house, it was the thing to do to listen to *"La Soirée de Hockey"* (Hockey Night) on television and watch René do the Canadiens' games.

For me, watching *"La Soirée de Hockey"* was a very important ritual that had to be performed just right. Before the game went on I would gather a bunch of pillows, place them on the floor in front of the TV set, and begin sweating. I took the games very seriously right from the start. In fact, I can remember the first game I ever saw. The Canadiens were playing the Toronto Maple Leafs in the Stanley Cup finals and, of course, I rooted for the Canadiens.

My rooting alone was very significant. The Montreal team, *les Canadiens,* represented French Canada, while the Maple Leafs were the team that English-speaking Canadians generally rooted for. The intensity of the rooting was kind of scary in retrospect. I hated the entire Toronto club—but especially their captain, George Armstrong, who was half Indian.

One reason for my deep feelings against Armstrong was the fact that he was skating against Jean Beliveau, the majestic center for the Canadiens. To French-Canadians, Beliveau represented the epitome of classic hockey playing. He was tall, strong, and exceptionally clean as a player. More than that, *le Gros Bill* (or Big Bill, as he was known) Beliveau did everything on the ice as it was written in hockey textbooks. He skated with long, firm strides. His shot was a black blur, usually right on the corner of the net, and he was completely unselfish with the puck. *Le Gros Bill* symbolized for French Canada what Rocket Richard had symbolized a decade earlier. As a result, anyone who skated opposite Beliveau immediately became my sworn enemy. Hence, I hated George Armstrong even though he was very much like Beliveau in stature and style (although hardly as smooth and competent).

Throughout the game, I would sit at the very edge of my pillows (Dad sat on a chair nearby), jumping up and down whenever *les Canadiens* scored. At that point René Lecavalier would utter the magic words: *"Beliveau lance . . . ET COMPTE!"* (Beliveau shoots . . . and scores!). The broadcasts had a profound influence on me. To this day, I still hate the Maple Leafs as a hockey club.

In my early days, our entire life was wrapped up in the French-Canadian culture. We lived in a neighborhood in which French was the only language spoken, although there were English-speaking communities in the immediate vicinity. Needless to say, we didn't get along all that well with our English-speaking neighbors. Our area was sort of a Gallic Archie Bunker's street, with all the houses looking alike—except for the color of the paint—and all the people thinking alike. To me, the whole world extended from my house to the end of the block; and that's all I cared about. The streets were usually empty of traffic, so we could play all the sports we wanted to right in front of the house—except for hockey which we'd play in the back.

Most of my playing, even at the age of four, was with older kids. I was afraid, in a way, to associate too closely with kids my own age. For one thing, they tended to cry a lot, and some were still wetting their beds. I was less of a cry-baby because I had terrific motivation. I knew that if I cried I wouldn't be accepted by Jean and his friends, so I conditioned myself not to cry. The fear of not being able to play hockey with the older guys was enough to drive me to do anything.

Likewise, I learned early on to tolerate the kind of injuries that would send other kids screaming for their parents. Once, during a game with my brother and his friends, I did get cut and it did hurt. But I wouldn't let go. I went into the house where my mother went along with the ritual. "Oh," she said, "it's just a little cut. Here comes our little workman." She patched me up and sent me back to the ice. My mother never made a big fuss over an injury and, naturally, I accepted that attitude because it fit in perfectly with my own plans. As a result, the fear of getting hurt never entered my mind.

But the fear of hurting *someone else* was always with me because I grew so fast and was always the strongest and biggest among those my age. I couldn't play with my brother's older friends all the time, so when I was with kids my age there was always a problem, especially in elementary school. We used to play a game called German Ball (a variation on dodgeball) where there are nine kids on each side and the idea is to throw the ball as fast as possible to the opponent, who has to catch it.

I wasn't a violent kid, but I was strong and I could whip that ball harder than anyone—by a lot! I would usually wind up hitting the kids in the face with the ball and hurting them. And as a result the kids my age didn't want to play with me, and I came off as some sort of tough guy. This bothered me because I didn't want to become known as a bully—yet I had a fanatical obsession with being the best.

This created quite a few problems for me and my parents. When I tossed a ball hard at another kid and accidentally hurt him, word would get back to my parents and I'd get the spanking of my life. Not once, not twice, but on a regular basis I would say, "Gee, I didn't mean to hurt him. It's not my fault. All I did was throw a ball hard and the kid couldn't handle it."

In a way I almost enjoyed the spankings, in that I felt they made me some sort of hero. I was five years old and my parents were concerned. They figured, There's the bully of the block and he loves it! Well, I was labelled a bully, there was no mistaking that. I had the image from the first day of class. All the other kids sat at normal desks, but for me they had to bring in a bigger desk because of my unusual size.

I was uncomfortable at first. There I was, sitting at a great big desk, all the other kids at tiny ones. But I began to get used to it; then I changed my attitude completely and became very proud of the difference. And it molded my philosophy. "If it makes me stand out," I figured, "it's good!" Size helped me gain respect from the others. I soon found that whatever I said to my classmates became the last word on the subject. I didn't have to punch anyone to get my point across, I only had to speak. It worked with just about everyone except one girl in our kindergarten class who also was quite big for her age.

What I really didn't like about her was her regular desire to plant kisses on my cheek. At that point in my life kissing was taboo. But she kept at it until I was fit to be tied, and I was determined to teach her a lesson that would straighten her out once and for all. One afternoon I got my chance. It was nap time and, like the other kids in the class, I put my head on the table as if I were taking a rest. But I had other ideas.

Inside my desk I had a building block in the shape of a gun. It was my weapon, and I was going to use it to "get" her. While the other kids were napping I took it out of my desk and sneaked toward her desk. The room was dark because the shades had been pulled down for nap time. Nobody noticed me and the teacher was out of the room.

I felt like I was acting out something from a John Wayne cowboy movie. I crawled up to my female nemesis and whacked her over the head with the wooden block. Knocked her right out!

Then I wheeled around and headed right back to my desk. By the time I got there a couple of girls were screaming, "She's dead! She's dead!"

When I heard that I began to feel a strange, queasy throb in my body, like I was starting to panic. I was afraid that I had really hurt her badly with that wooden block. Actually, the girl soon recovered, but I was hauled into the principal's office for a real tongue-lashing. Worse still, Mum was called in by the principal.

Having my mother called before the head of our school was more humiliating to our family than anything else, and I paid the price for it that night. I took a far worse beating than the girl had had from me that day. My parents wouldn't let me sit down to the table and have supper with them. I had to kneel in the corner on the wooden floor throughout the evening. The only bite I had to eat was a crumb of bread that Jean tossed me while I was kneeling.

I learned from that experience. There was the warning from the principal that any more of that nonsense and I'd be in real trouble at school. Worse, there was the threat that my parents would punish me by keeping me away from hockey if I didn't behave. More than anything, that kept me in line—the fear that I wouldn't be able to play if I misbehaved.

And if I couldn't play, it meant I couldn't pretend to be like my idol, Jean Beliveau. But the interesting thing is that even though I thought there was nobody else in the world but Beliveau, I always felt that I really wanted to be Denis Potvin first and that I wanted Denis Potvin to become as accomplished and important as Jean Beliveau.

To be honest, I soon became a glory-seeker. I began to fight and push to make my name known, and I soon realized that the best way to accomplish that was through sports—and hockey in particular. I knew that everyone liked athletes; people always talked about them. If I played well, they'd talk about me. Of course, being a kid, I was still very impressionable. At times I'd think it'd be great to be short and skinny; then I could skate faster and more gracefully. After mulling over the thought for a while, I'd come to the conclusion that wanting to be someone else wasn't right. Inevitably, I'd come to the same conclusion: I want to be Denis Potvin. And I want to be number one.

It wasn't just in hockey, either. I remember trying out once for the local football team when I was only about six or seven. I showed up at the park for a tryout and the coach looked me over, up and down. "You look big and strong," he said. "You should do very well on the line."

I think most kids would have accepted the coach's decision without a comeback. Not me. "No, sir," I said, "I want to play fullback. I want to carry the ball. I want to be the hero."

I learned that such assertiveness paid off. I got to be fullback and I loved it, mostly because of the challenge to do better. The first time I stepped on the football field my instinct was to look around, find the biggest guy on the opposition, and say to myself, I'm going to knock him down. I always wanted someone bigger. The bigger my victim, the better it was for my ego.

You have to remember that I grew up speaking French in an English-speaking country. Only about a quarter of Canada's 23 million people are French-speaking, and most of them are crammed into the province of Quebec. We lived in the shadow of the English-speaking capital of the country, Ottawa. In that sense, I think I had an added motivation to make good because there was always some kind of episode to remind me of my heritage.

A lot of the French-speaking kids from my neighborhood used to play football and baseball on Rue Vincent Massey, a little street separating the English and the French sections of town. We French kids would have a game of football going and the English guys would come over and interfere with our game. Or I'd bicycle over to Rue Vincent Massey and, if an English kid happened to notice me and knew I was French, he'd throw something at me. There was constant aggression between the two groups. I was never really into street-fighting, though I did find that my size made it important that I didn't turn away from a battle.

The thing that kept me going was the way French kids my age depended on me. (They didn't know how scared *I* was, and I wasn't about to let on to them, either.) Mostly I was frightened about the *stupidity* of getting hurt on the street in a senseless way—as opposed to getting hurt on the ball field. Athletic "violence" made sense to me, so I was never afraid of swinging hockey sticks, sharp skate-blades, or fast-flying pucks. But once we walked out onto the street, I was inwardly afraid, and I only fought out of sheer fear and self-protection.

Unfortunately, there were times when I couldn't avoid a confrontation with English-speaking bullies. They commonly used such derogatory slang expressions for us as "Pepsi" and "Frog." And if any English-speaking kid called a French kid a name like that, there was always a good chance that he was asking for a fight.

There was a pattern to these incidents: an insult along ethnic lines, a response, then blows. I was walking to the Dairy Queen one time with a couple of friends when the English guys opened up. They'd start with the "Froggie" routine, then there'd be pushing, then fighting. We'd fight and fight and fight until we got tired. Then we'd get up and walk home.

No matter what the result of the fight, my reactions immediately afterwards were always the same: I had to get home and shape myself up so that neither of my parents—but especially my dad—knew what had happened. So, after a fight, I would come home, go straight down to the basement, and try to clean myself up. Needless to say, I never talked about the battles with my folks. I knew that they felt fighting wasn't right.

The battles, to put them in perspective, were a very minor conflict in my early years. The major conflict was between hockey and school. My parents, having come from a lower-middle-class environment, were very anxious for me to get as much education as possible. Not only did Dad want me to do well in school, he also had this very strong feeling about sports, and especially hockey. He was very proud of my athletic ability, just as he had been with Jean and Bob before me. But he also wanted me to do well in school, and that's where I disappointed my parents.

I might have been a good student had not everything in my life come to revolve around hockey by the time I was six. My interest in hockey even then reached such an intense level that friends of our family were worried that I would quit school and concentrate only on hockey. They'd tell my folks about the stereotyped hockey player of that era— big, fast, and dumb—who left school after Grade Three. And it worried them.

So all I'd hear was constant harping about staying in school and studying, to the point where I really got to hate the books—except for history and science. When I applied myself to those subjects I did well. By "apply," I mean that I made a point of playing hockey first and finding room for homework afterwards. Usually I did my "homework" every morning in school before my first class.

Looking back, I'm sure Dad's obsession with my schooling was rooted in his own misfortune with the Red Wings. We'd be sitting at the dinner table and he'd tell me about the injury he suffered at the Detroit training camp. "You can never tell what's going to happen to you on the ice," he'd say. "Look at me, one injury and I could never play pro again. Denis, it could happen to you, too."

I took Dad very seriously when he talked about the accident. But in all honesty very little of what he said seeped through. When I walked away from the table it was as if I were walking away from his thoughts. They were gone and were replaced by my own ideas. I kept thinking, Hey, that can't happen to me. It happens to other guys but not to me.

Consequently, I never worried about getting hurt in a game. I always figured that any injured limb in my body would be repairable and that nothing could keep young Denis Potvin down.

# THE BROTHERS POTVIN

Through the years there have been a number of successful brother acts in the National Hockey League. Early in the century the Patrick Brothers, Lester and Frank, operated the Pacific Coast League and wrote many of the rules that are part of the modern game. Years later Lester's sons, Murray and Lynn, teamed together on the New York Rangers. In Chicago the Black Hawks had Max and Doug Bentley skating on a forward line. And, of course, Maurice and Henri Richard played side by side for the Montreal Canadiens. But, as far as I'm concerned, there never has been an NHL brother act quite like The Brothers Potvin of the Islanders.

The tight brotherly bond between Jean and me was cemented at a very early age. For years we spent our summers together at the family cottage on the Ottawa River about 20 miles from home. And it was real country living. We were isolated on a dirt road, alone but for one other home nearby. We were surrounded by trees, a river, a swamp, and lots of rabbits, frogs, and snakes.

One of Jean's favorite pastimes at the cottage was tree-climbing, a sport that might have cost him his life had I not, by a stroke of luck, been around at the time and at the base of the tree.

This particular tree was exceptionally high—at least it looked high to me—and surrounded by a huge flat rock at its base. Jean seemed oblivious to the danger as he climbed higher and higher, doing a French-Canadian imitation of Jack climbing the beanstalk.

Meanwhile, there was little Denis at the bottom, looking up as Jean disappeared among the branches and leaves. As a five-year-old I could only estimate the height of the tree, but I imagined that it was at least 50 feet high.

As I peered through the branches, trying to follow Jean's upward movement, I was startled by a strange sound, then another and another, each louder and scarier. I realized that it was the sound of branches breaking. I looked directly above me and saw branch after branch break away. Then, out of the mass of leaves and branches, came Jean crashing down, heading directly for the rock below.

Without thinking about the consequences—there really was no time to think—I instinctively held out my arms. To my utter amazement, he plopped right into them, and I held him for a split second, long enough to break his fall and insure his safety.

When he finally reached the ground, I could see that he had been through a terrible trauma. His body was scratched from head to toe and he was bawling his head off. By this time my parents had raced out of the house; we all comforted Jean and then took him to the hospital just to be sure that nothing serious had happened to him. Thanks to my lucky arms, nothing had been damaged but his designs on climbing the Himalayas.

If trees thereafter gave Jean a bit of a fright, dogs became my nemesis as a result of a terribly scary episode at the same cottage. As I said, there was only one other home nearby, and we were quite friendly with the family who lived there; so friendly, in fact, that I thought nothing of going over there to play with their dog, a huge German shepherd.

After a while, I had become friendly with the old gal and I felt the shepherd was friendly with me. But I made the mistake of continuing the friendship with her pups too soon after they were born. I strolled over one day, saw the pups, and picked one up in my arms and began fondling it.

All I remember is hearing a growl, seeing the protective mother leap at my throat, and feeling a claw at my eye. I closed my eye just in time and escaped with what seemed to be a very bloody eye, but the blood was streaming from the ripped flesh directly *above* the eye itself. Having done the damage, the dog became calm, but I didn't. My screams brought the family rescue team and, like Jean, I was taken to the hospital and put to sleep while several stitches were sewn above the eye. To this day, when I see a dog, I get a little leery and give it a wide berth.

Obviously, Jean and I never in our wildest dreams imagined that we would play on the same NHL team at the same time, skating together on a power play and shooting for a league record. How could we? When Jean and I were growing up in Ottawa the NHL was still a tight six-team league with only two Canadian clubs and little prospect of expansion.

That didn't prevent us from dreaming about making it to the top; so dream we did, and we played every single day that ice was available. Our first experience together in organized hockey came when we were both still in elementary school. Jean was in Grade Eight and I was in Grade Four. I was eight years old and Jean was 12. Though I was four years younger than Jean, I was big enough and good enough to play with the older fellows on the school team.

Our age difference never mattered in those days. In fact, it was never a factor in our communicating with each other until he began dating girls. But, even though we did communicate, my personal feelings toward Jean were not free and easy. I felt very anxious about playing with him because I desperately wanted to impress my older brother and I wanted to do better than, or at least as well as, Jean.

The big guys weren't so quick to let me play with them, and that's where Jean was a big help. He'd tell off the big fellows and make sure that I got into the games. None of this would have been possible if I hadn't been able to play up to their level, but I was, and the competition didn't bother me until we stepped off the ice. Then I felt hurt because these same guys that I skated with completely ignored me away from the rink.

That's where the five-year age difference really had an impact. I felt equal to them in sports, so I assumed I should be their equal on a social level. Instead, I was pushed into a corner and ignored. The message came through loud and clear: They weren't my friends, just my teammates. When they went off to the dances with the girls, Denis went to the ice cream parlor and had a malted.

Jean didn't interfere in any of my business unless he felt he really had to, and I respected his intuition, especially after one incident in which a high school kid really laid me out, and right on my own front lawn!

It happened one day right after school. I was walking home, minding my business, when a couple of English-speaking high school kids came the other way. I must have been daydreaming at the time because I didn't even noice them and just blindly bumped into this older guy.

"I'm sorry," I said in my broken English, and I just figured that he would accept my casual apology without a second thought. But I was wrong.

The big guy looked down at me and let me have a haymaker of a punch right in the face. Talk about seeing stars, I really saw them for about five seconds after his fist met my head. I collapsed to the ground, covering myself with my arms for protection. I was scared, partly because of the surprise and partly because of his fury, which I couldn't understand.

None of this would have been terribly tragic except that I was face down on the grass of our own front lawn. Worse, brother Jean just happened to have been sitting by the window in the house and saw the entire episode.

Once I was down, and apparently out, the English kid just walked away with his chums. I was humiliated, though I still wasn't aware that Jean had seen the guy belt me out. I dusted myself off and slinked into the house, hoping against hope that nobody would be around. But Jean walked down the stairs, looked at me, and shook his head in disgust. It was obvious from the look in his eyes that he had seen what had happened and was teed off at me for taking the abuse without retaliating.

Jean was really bothered by what he saw. Looking back, I'm sure he decided then to help me in the future if a similar situation developed. I guess Jean figured the best way to solve the problem was to get some advice from Dad. When my father came home from work that night Jean told him what had happened to me on the front lawn.

My father was obviously disturbed by what Jean told him. He called me over for a heart-to-heart talk, the kind my father and I had rarely had before. "Listen," he said as sternly as I could ever remember him speak, "I never want you to start a fight. But if anyone ever starts up with you, no matter how big the guy may be, *I never want you to back down from a battle. Never again!*"

The point was made—maybe too well. As I grew older, I filled out more quickly than anyone in the neighborhood. At the age of ten I was 5'8" tall and weighed 130 pounds, and by the time I was 14 I had reached 185 pounds.

A lot of people couldn't believe that I was as young as I was. In order to prove my age to the various athletic leaders, I had reproductions made of my birth certificate. But I had the hardest time proving it to some of the parents of my opponents.

One mother tried to have me barred from a football league I played in. I was too big, she argued, to be within the age limits; besides, I was manhandling her son, who played for the other team. Granted, I had hit him pretty hard during a "mosquito" league game, but I figured she got carried away with her response.

Before I knew what was happening, the woman had run out on the field and grabbed me by the neck with more force than the best tackle on her son's team. It was all I could do to fight her off when the kid's coach came out to join her. Once that happened, *my* father came running out on the field and jumped in. Pretty soon, the scene began to look like an old Marx Brothers movie.

It's an unfortunate aspect of kids' sports that parents sometimes get too deeply involved in the games from their vantage point in the stands. As I grew older, I began to notice how Mum and Dad became tense during any game in which Jean or I was playing. Sometimes the scene got rather violent, as on the night I played in a tournament at Cornwall, Ontario, not far from our home in Ottawa.

About 3,000 fans were in the rink that night, and they weren't rooting for our team. The fact that I happened to be having a particularly good night seemed to annoy a lot of the Cornwall fans, especially one loudmouthed guy who berated me at the top of his lungs almost from the opening face-off. There wasn't a name in the book that he didn't call me and he even threw in a few of his own invention for good measure.

What the loudmouth didn't realize was that the rather big, red-haired woman (with a temper to match her fiery red hair) who stood directly in front of him was growing angrier by the second. Finally, Mister Loudmouth uttered one expletive too many about Denis Potvin, and my mother wheeled around and—thwack!—punched him right in the face. She hit the guy so hard he was stunned. Fortunately, my father came over and ushered my mother away from the ice. I happened to see the entire battle from ice level, thinking to myself, Mum's got a terrific right cross.

I wasn't surprised at my mother's reaction because I knew how deeply emotional she could be and how invested she felt in my hockey career. After all, from the very start she and Dad would be up at four or five on winter mornings to take me to practice or tournaments. Whenever we went on the road for an All-Star game she would chaperone, usually with Dad at the side.

Both of them helped me to develop an immunity to pain simply by discouraging my complaints. I'd get high-sticked on the ice, come home, show them the wound, and—if it really was a big or deep one—I'd cry or whimper. Dad would snap at me, "Oh, stop crying, it's going to heal." And that would be that. They played down the injuries so much that I soon learned to brush them off like mosquitoes on my wrist.

I also realized early on that it was useless to argue with my dad or raise my voice against him. He was the dominant personality in our house, and if he told me to brush off an injury, I had no choice but to brush it off and make the best of it.

This was more easily said than done. After all, I felt frustration as much as the next person. And I had to have an outlet if I couldn't express my anger against my father. To relieve my aggression, I would head straight for the basement after a lecture and punch the hell out of my pillow. I'd make believe that the pillow was my dad and I'd swing away until I got all of my fury out of my system.

I don't mean to suggest that Dad singled me out for punishment in our house. Jean got his share, too, sometimes deservedly and sometimes when he didn't rate the whacks. Both Jean and I were out quite late once on a Friday night, far beyond our curfew limit (which was something like midnight).

Dad didn't realize that night that I was out, but he knew that Jean had a date. When either of us was out past curfew time, my father would wait up for the culprit to come home, like a sentry on duty. On this particular Friday, Jean walked in at about one in the morning—and all hell broke loose.

Jean walked in the front door, which was his first mistake; Dad was right there waiting for him. "Why can't you take better care of yourself?" Dad shouted. "You're a hockey player and you shouldn't be messing around, staying out late like this."

This time Dad did more than shout; he gave Jean quite a beating, and when he got through my big brother walked downstairs with tears in his eyes. In the basement, he went to my room to commiserate with me and found my bed still freshly made—which meant only one thing: I still hadn't come home.

I didn't get home until four in the morning, when I sneaked in through the basement and went right to bed. Jean was fast asleep and didn't hear me come into the room. When he got up in the morning he told me about the beating he had gotten and how angry Dad had been. I figured I was in *big* trouble.

I quaked in my boots as I approached the breakfast table with Jean. Mum and Dad were already there when we sat down. There was a minute or two of silence at first. Obviously they were still angry with Jean. Nobody said a word to him. But soon they began talking and joking with *me* like I couldn't believe. Of course, Jean could have spoiled it by telling them how late I had come in, but Jean wasn't the type of brother who would snitch, and I got away with my late-night escapade.

What I had going for me was my age. Because I was the youngest of three boys, I got special treatment in many ways. It happened the first time my dad caught me smoking. I was about 12 then and, like all kids my age, I had a big curiosity about smoking. Since the older guys did it, I felt it was something I ought to do, too. I used to walk along the streets with my friends, picking up cigarette butts, lighting them, and taking a few puffs. I didn't want my parents to know that I had smoked, so when I got home I'd brush my teeth as hard as I could, thinking the toothpaste would cover up the smoke on my breath and my folks wouldn't know I had touched cigarettes.

I got a little more brazen one day and actually brought a cigarette into our house, not knowing that my father was around. I went to my room, enjoyed inhaling, and felt pretty good about the experience. Unfortunately, the smell of smoke lingered. When Dad came downstairs a while later, he soon realized what had happened.

"You've had a puff, haven't you?" he asked, staring me down pretty hard.

I told him I had. I expected the kind of belting Dad had given Jean the night Jean came home after midnight.

But my father really faked me out. "Denis," he said very calmly and with paternal affection, "smoking isn't good for you."

That was it. I thought he'd kill me for taking a puff, and all I got were a few words of advice. Now, in retrospect, I realize that I never should have started smoking in the first place. Dad was right!

There has been a myth going the rounds for many years that every Canadian kid dreams of playing someday in the National Hockey League. It assumes that every kid in Canada loves hockey, which really isn't the case. But hockey *is* our national sport, and a healthy percentage of the youngsters I grew up with had their eyes and hearts on the NHL. For me the turning point was a game at the old Ottawa Auditorium when I was only seven years old.

The Auditorium (we called it The Aud) was an ancient building that once was home for the Ottawa NHL team that folded in the early thirties. Years later Ottawa had a club in the old Quebec Senior Hockey League that became notorious as the team that played in the old egg-shaped rink. The Aud did have an egg shape about it, compared to the normal rectangular form of all other rinks.

On this night my father took me to see the Montreal Canadiens play a junior amateur club called the Montreal Junior Canadiens. Seeing the Canadiens was, corny as it may sound, a dream come true. They skated out on the milky white ice wearing their traditional *bleu, blanc, et rouge* (blue, white, and red) uniforms with the large C crest (with an H in the middle of the C) on the front of the jerseys. We all knew that it meant *Club de Hockey Canadien.*

Dad and I sat in the very top row; I felt that anything higher would have been in Heaven. I *was* in Heaven, seeing such stars as Henri Richard, Jean Beliveau, Doug Harvey, Dickie Moore, and the great Jacques Plante in goal. Even from our seat at the top we could hear Plante screaming instructions to his defensemen. Of course the NHL club won the game easily, but that wasn't as much a kick to me as what happened after the game.

My father and I went downstairs to the Canadiens' dressing room in hopes of getting a glimpse of the players. We knew it wasn't going to be easy, but we were lucky: We knew the guy who ran the skate shop next to the dressing room, and he made sure that I got into a decent position when the players came out.

It became very crowded and, since I was still quite small, I couldn't see over the shoulders of the adults. I really couldn't make out any of the stars until this one player came out, a guy I wasn't all that familiar with, but a Canadien nonetheless. A few people were around him as I approached and asked for his autograph.

He sure wasn't Jean Beliveau or Henri Richard, but I trembled with expectation as he put his hand on my shoulder. Then I realized that it wasn't an affectionate pat at all; he pushed me aside and walked away, out the door and into the night. It was my first experience of trying to get an autograph—and my last.

Perhaps a keener disappointment in early years was one when I played for our neighborhood team, Overbrook, which was coached by my father. Armand Potvin was a dedicated father and an equally dedi-cated coach. It was a wonderful combination, except that Dad worked so hard at it that he became, in effect, a 24-hour coach to me. He'd coach me at practices and when we got home he'd coach me at night. He was very involved, and there were times when I wished he were a *booster* rather than a coach.

This father-son, coach-son relationship lasted only a year, after which Dad gave up coaching. Although he was intensely interested in my growth as a hockey player, Armand Potvin made a point never to interfere with subsequent coaches I played under, from my early days right up to junior hockey.

Like most kids our age, we always seemed to be looking ahead to the next team and, at that time, the best next team around was an outfit called Altavista. The really good players on Overbrook wanted to graduate to Altavista because it was backed by a very wealthy man who would buy the very best equipment for his kids and take them on all sorts of exotic trips to play in out-of-town tournaments.

Late in the season a gifted young skater named Steven and I were invited to join the Altavista team. At that point in our lives it was like getting an invitation to play for the Canadiens. Altavista had just accepted an invitation to play in a big peewee tournament at Quebec City that was the very best of all peewee championships, sort of like the Stanley Cup playoffs for young Canadians. I thought that the invitation was the greatest thing that had happened to me in or out of hockey.

Steven quickly accepted the invitation, obtained permission from his father, and "jumped" from Overbrook to the Altavista team. I went home that night and told my father that I had been asked to play for the rich team. I told him how I would be going to Quebec City, to stay at the huge Château Frontenac Hotel and play before 14,000 people every night.

"You can't go!" my father shot back.

I couldn't believe my ears.

"You can't go," my father reiterated, "because you'd be letting down every one of your teammates on Overbrook. That's where your obligation is, not with this big-deal Altavista team with the fancy uniforms and expensive skates. It isn't right for you to leave a team in mid-season."

I wanted to jump out the window, I was so mad. I couldn't understand his reasoning and I couldn't have disagreed with him more. But, at the same time, I knew that I had no choice but to accept his decision. I was bitter and angry with my father and I held it against him for quite some time—at least until Steven came back from Quebec. He tried to return to Overbrook and was scorned by everyone, barred from playing *all* sports in Overbrook. In time I realized that Dad was right.

Another disappointment to me in my earlier years was my high school history teacher. By chance, he also happened to be coach of our school hockey team and a guy, I figured, who had an appreciation of my talents.

But somehow he always seemed to be discouraging me from playing hockey, and I never could quite figure out why. Possibly it was because I also happened to be a pretty good football player and he thought I might do better on the gridiron. In any event, I reached a point where I was playing hockey out of school but wasn't satisfied that I was getting enough ice time, so I tried out for the high school varsity.

Unfortunately, I had pulled a muscle in my back during a football game and was still a little sore when the hockey tryouts began. We worked out for a week, until there were 25 kids on the squad. "I have to make five cuts," the coach told us. "These will be the last. Everyone else makes the team."

That didn't bother me because I was sure I was better than most of the other guys, if not all of them. But I began to have my doubts when the teacher invited me to his office for a meeting. "Denis," he said, "I'm really sorry, but I don't think we'll be able to use you this year. Maybe next season."

"Why?" I asked.

"You're too slow," he said. "There are big guys that you can't seem to handle. You need another year of hard work and then maybe you'll get quicker and better. I hope that you'll come out for the team next year."

I was shocked, stunned right to the core. Nothing like this had ever happened to me before. Not only was I rejected, but I was also being dumped from a high school team which played in a very low-level league. That history teacher would live to regret his decision, I vowed— and there was nothing more I could do.

"Fine," I told him, "I'll do my best." I bit my lip, held back my anger, and went home.

I would have been thoroughly destroyed if I hadn't already proven myself on other teams. But I had graduated from the Overbrook team and was now asked a second time to join Altavista. This time Dad agreed to let me skate with them. I had fulfilled my obligation to the neighborhood club, and he felt I was good enough to play with the best.

Playing for Altavista was big stuff. We had nice, shiny jackets and pants, the very best equipment, and all the trappings of a major league team. For its level it was the most prestigious team in Ottawa—and, not surprisingly, one of the most disliked clubs in the area.

After the rejection by my high school coach, playing for Altavista was just what I needed. I played well for them, and I knew that scouts for the junior team in town, the Ottawa 67s, who used us as a farm team, were scouting us all the time. And, despite what my history teacher had said, I knew I was playing damn good hockey for a 13-year-old.

For me, the biggest ego boost of all would have been an invitation to try out with the 67s. Training camp started in September, but I never got an invitation to try out. (Jean had already been skating with them for a few years, which made it an even greater disappointment.) I did the best I could with Altavista and hoped for recognition the following season.

The months went by, September, October, November, December, and I was getting better each time I played for Altavista. I was 13 but had the physique of a person ten years older, and I felt that I was beginning to think like an adult hockey player.

One evening in January the family was sitting around the dinner table, eating chicken with rice, when the phone rang. I had just gulped down a piece of chicken and Jean's mouth was empty, so he picked up the receiver. For some instinctive reason I watched him closely as he talked.

"Hi, how're ya doin'?" Jean said. Then he stood up, smiled, and turned toward me. "Okay, I'll tell him." And he hung up.

"Who was it?" I demanded.

Jean smiled a proud smile and told me it had been Bill Long, coach of the Ottawa 67s. "Denis, he wants you at the rink tonight."

I pushed the dinner plate away, dressed, and ran all the way to the rink. Long was there. He was a very respected coach in the Ontario Hockey Association's Junior A Division and had had lots of experience coaching the best teen-age players in Canada. In fact, Long had once coached the Niagara Falls Flyers, the team that sent Derek Sanderson, Gilles Marotte, and Bernie Parent to the NHL, so he was pretty well known across the country. I felt I was in good hands.

What was really ironic about the whole thing was that not only was my opening game against this same Niagara Falls team, but I both survived the game and got a write-up in the paper. The story was about this 13-year-old kid who was going to be "the next Bobby Orr." When I walked into my history class the next day my teacher had the clipping up on his bulletin board.

I saw the clipping and felt awfully proud; after all, this was the coach who had said I wasn't good enough to make the high school team. "I'm really sorry I couldn't make your team," I said to him with a straight face. "Does this mean I have another chance now?"

Now the question was just how far I could go with the 67s. I finished the season with them and played well enough for a 13-year-old to know I'd be invited back to training camp the following fall. But I still had my eyes set on big-time football.

For in many ways football was my first love. I loved the crunch of body against body and the great feel of the outdoors. There was something special about football that appealed to me, and that was the romance of going to an American university like UCLA. Remember, this was the mid-sixties and UCLA, to a kid from Ottawa, was the most glamorous school in college football. I'd watch the games on TV, hear the roar of 100,000 people in the stands, catch the spirit of the cheerleaders, and feel terribly excited. I thought it would be great to have all those people standing and cheering Denis Potvin.

At first I thought I could combine both a football and a hockey career. A Canadian named Gerry James did it in the late fifties. He played football for the Winnipeg Blue Bombers and then, when the season was over, he skated for the Toronto Maple Leafs. If James could manage to combine the two sports for a few seasons, why not Denis Potvin?

I got the answer right away from my football coach Gene Robillard. I told him my plan: I'd miss a couple of hockey practices to get in the football games, but I'd also have to miss a few football scrimmages to get in my hockey games. "Look, Mr. Robillard," I reasoned, "the football games are in the afternoon and the hockey games are at night. I'll go from one game to the other."

Robillard, a real disciplinarian, just shook his head. "I don't want you to miss *any* practices. You have to make a decision: Either play hockey or play football. But not both."

It was a difficult decision. My heart was still with football, but my intuition led me to hockey because it had a longer season and I knew the money would be better.

I never played football again and, to this day, I have second thoughts about the decision. I loved football and I miss it a lot.

But I had made my decision; now it was a matter of making a name for myself on the ice.

# JOUSTING IN THE JUNIOR LEAGUES

Hitting has always been an important part of my repertoire, first as a football player and then on the ice, playing defense. When I played football I never enjoyed running around the end as much as I did bashing my way right through the middle of the line. It wasn't just hitting but getting hit as well that seemed to give me such tremendous physical pleasure. After I quit football I found a similar thrill on the ice going into the corners, feeling the crunch of body against body, stick against stick. In a purely impersonal sense, I enjoyed hurting people with my body, as long as they weren't seriously injured.

That was one of the differences between Jean and me. He never had a mean streak when he was on the ice, and I think that aspect of his play hurt him; he was never a hitter. In fact, the only time Jean did any hitting, it seemed, was when one of the big guys on the opposition went after *me*. It was a throwback to the days when Henri Richard was a rookie on the Montreal Canadiens. Every time a big defenseman such as Lou Fontinato of the New York Rangers took a run at Henri, his big brother Maurice would go charging into Fontinato to protect his kid brother.

So, if somebody took a run at Denis Potvin, Jean would be right on the guy's back, giving it to him. It was very embarrassing at first because it looked as though I couldn't take care of myself. I realized that Jean was doing his bit out of a sense of brotherliness, so I took him aside and said, "Hey, brother, let me fight my own battles."

Since then, Jean has let me stand on my own two skates—which wasn't very easy at first. Remember, I was only 13 years old, playing in a league with guys as old as 20. It was a league that many writers considered *tougher* than the NHL and one in which a man had to establish his *machismo* bright and early, even if he was a 13-year-old "man."

One reason for my confidence was the karate course I had started taking. I soon became fairly adept at it, to the point of entering competition. But what exercise and feeling of vitality I enjoyed doing karate came *only* as a sport. It is almost physically impossible to adapt karate moves to the ice rink, and I had no intention of doing so.

Trouble on the ice has to be handled in a more rudimentary way: with fists.

Naturally, there are as many sources of trouble as there are hockey teams—especially a hockey team that has Dave Schultz as a winger. I was still a member of the 67s when I had my first encounter with Mister Schultz, who was then a Philadelphia Flyers farmhand, playing for the Richmond Robins. We played against the Robins in an exhibition game, and I got a taste of "The Hammer's" style first-hand.

I'd be on the ice and Schultz would be on the bench, incessantly carping at me, "I'm gonna get you, Potvin, I'm gonna get you, Potvin!" At first it worried me. I'd take quick glimpses over my shoulder toward his bench to see whether he was coming out on the ice. It wasn't so much a matter of being scared as it was of preparing myself for what might happen, like a sneak attack from the rear. I didn't want to get suckered, and I knew from my teammates that Schultz was the kind of guy who would hit from behind.

Finally we had our confrontation. There was a bit of a ruckus near the boards involving some guys who were fighting and then wrestling (the usual pattern to a hockey fight finds the guys dropping their gloves, throwing punches, and winding up in a wrestling embrace) and I ended up holding some opponent in the corner. In the back of my mind I had a feeling Schultz might pull some nonsense with me, so I let go of the guy I had grappled with to be on guard for "The Hammer." As I turned around, I came face to face with Schultz, with the referee and a couple of players between us.

Schultz immediately began jabbering away at me, and I gave him some lip right back across the mass of humanity. Then, all of a sudden, something snapped inside me. I blew my cool and hurled my glove at him. "Let's go!" I demanded, inviting him to fight. But by then the officials had made sure that nothing more would happen, and we were both escorted to the penalty box with a pair of minor two-minute penalties for roughing.

I knew why Schultz was mad at me. I was playing a hitting game. Even though I was one of the youngest players in the league I hit everyone in sight, and I was catching guys at center ice with pretty solid shoulder and hip checks. When a guy gets hit with one of those checks, he's bound to get angry. In fact some of my own teammates would get angry with me when I'd throw the same kind of check in practice. One teammate, Connie Forey, who also knew I was taking karate lessons at the time, walked over to my dressing room stall one day and started giving me all kinds of lip. He wound it up by saying, "Karate isn't gonna help you around this dressing room."

I jumped to my feet and shouted back at him, "Okay, Connie, let's find out." But our coach, Bill Long, was there when it happened and he rushed in to make sure I didn't give any karate demonstrations to my teammates.

By the time I was 15, I had developed as much skill in karate as I felt I should. I didn't want to take advantage of the martial art while I was on the ice. But I felt confident that I could handle myself if any of the goons on the opposition gave me grief.

And there were plenty of roughnecks roaming the Ontario Hockey Association in those days. Perhaps the roughest of all was Steve Durbano, who later played for a number of NHL teams including the St. Louis Blues, the Pittsburgh Penguins, and the Colorado Rockies.

As a junior, Durbano was capable of anything and everything. Once, out with a leg injury, I watched him from the stands and observed Durbano's tactics.

In the first battle, Durbano took on Brian MacSheffrey of our club. Brian was an easygoing guy, not prone to getting into violent tiffs. But this time he gave Durbano as much as Steve gave him and he came out of it with dignity and no severe injury. That was early in the game. Later, MacSheffrey reappeared on the ice and I noticed him briefly and turned away. When I glanced back, there was MacSheffrey, lying in the corner, bleeding like a stuck pig. He had been speared with the pointed blade of a stick. Brian was rushed to the hospital by ambulance and barely survived. Another inch and Brian would have been dead.

Another time Durbano nearly took off Peter Laframboise's leg at the ankle in a playoff game in which Durbano skated for the Toronto Marlboros. Peter was standing in front of the net when Durbano rushed him from behind. Whack! Durbano slashed him on the ankle so hard that we actually heard the crack where we were sitting on the bench.

Virtually the same thing happened to a kid named Mike Bloom who beat up Durbano. Just one period later Bloom paid the price for it when

Durbano came charging out on the ice and cross-checked Bloom across the face, breaking his nose.

The question is, of course, How does one survive against characters like Durbano? The key word is vigilance. When they are on the ice, I make a point of knowing that they're there, and if I'm carrying the puck and skating toward them, I'm careful to let them make the first move. Frequently they will charge out and I'll just swerve around them and make my play on goal.

The real problem in dealing with a roughneck player comes when I go after the puck in the corner of the rink. I know that at any second he's liable to skate in, his stick at bayonet level, ready to spear me. I have to keep myself as psyched up as possible and, if he hits me, give it right back. Once I give it back I know he won't bother me again. That's how you have to get respect.

Brother Jean got respect from Durbano when both were playing junior hockey. It happened in Ottawa when Durbano was playing in the Ontario Hockey Association.

He did not scare Jean.

Durbano made three mistakes: he fouled Jean, he squared off against my brother, and he failed to scout Jean as a boxer and didn't discover that my brother is a southpaw swinger and not a righthander.

The result was gory and embarrassing for Steve.

Before Durbano could launch his first jab, Jean, the lefty, smashed Steve in the nose and Durbano went down, blood oozing from his proboscis. He was finally escorted from the ice, leaving a crimson trail. Having been right next to Durbano when it started, I enjoyed a ringside seat for the TKO. And it was a gratifying sight, not because Jean won the fight, but because Durbano got his comeuppance. Durbano has never bothered my brother again.

Sometimes the fans were more difficult than our opponents in junior hockey. You hear a lot of talk about how The Forum in Montreal is the shrine of all Canadian arenas and, in a sense, that is because of its age (it's the oldest building in the NHL) and heritage. But the junior hockey fans who peopled The Forum when I played for Ottawa were really rough when they felt that their team, the Junior Canadiens, were getting a raw deal.

One night we gave them a raw deal and it brought out the Montreal police riot squad. In those days the Junior Canadiens were considered the class amateur team of French Canada. They had young aces such as

Gil Perreault, Richard Martin, Réjean Houle, and Marc Tardif. To beat a club like that you really had to be on your game, and on this night we were. The score was 6–4 in our favor late in the game when the fans began getting uptight.

The Montreal Forum is designed in such a way that the fans can walk behind the players' bench. A regular aisle runs immediately adjacent to the area in which the team sits. While the game was still on, a fan charged down the aisle, punched Connie Forey, then wheeled around and dashed up the stairs toward the top of the rink.

Forey was stunned momentarily. Recovering he took off after the fan, skates and all. Roy Green, our spare goaltender, had seen the whole episode and, thinking Forey wouldn't recover so quickly, with his big, fat pads and 40 pounds of goaltending equipment ran up the stairs after the guy, too.

The partisan Montreal fans didn't like this one bit, and they swarmed down on Green in waves. They were mauling him by their sheer number and carrying him to higher ground so that more fans could move in and toss punches. From the bench we could see that Roy was in real danger, so we went to his rescue. Soon it seemed everyone in the rink around us was fighting.

We finally got Roy and Connie free, and our coach, Bill Long, hustled us to the dressing room while the fans kept swinging at anyone in a 67s uniform. About 40 wild-eyed fans surrounded our dressing room door when we got there, and they all seemed to be screaming unpleasant things at us.

It wasn't easy getting into the dressing room because there were only two policemen trying to handle the crowd. One guy jumped right out of the crowd, lunged at my stick, and tried to grab me. I put the point of the stick at his stomach and shouted, "To get to me you'll have to go past five feet of lumber!"

Fans swung at us before we could get into the room, and to protect ourselves we had to swing back, clipping a few of them pretty good about the shoulders. By now the riot squad had arrived and we made it safely into the room and, later, out of the building.

Not all rivalries were as nasty as that. I had a wonderful one-on-one rivalry with my present teammate, Billy Harris, who was then skating for the Toronto Marlboros. As a junior, Billy was a big scorer and eventually became the top draft pick in all Canada and the first selection made by the Islanders. His assets were his accurate shot and his great physical strength together with an extraordinary skating balance. Once

Billy had made a move around the flanks, it was almost impossible to stop him.

Since Billy and I developed at virtually the same time, we created what amounted to a rivalry of skills, and every time our teams would meet we would challenge each other, almost by instinct. I think he respected my abilities and I know that I respected his.

I remember once he skated down on me, one-on-one, shifted to the left, and then crossed me up by swerving sharply to the right. Then he moved in on our goalie and scored. It was terribly embarrassing for me and I made a mental note not to let that happen again.

Not long after, Harris got the puck again and began churning his legs like a wild man. He went one way and I went with him. Then he tried to shift direction, but I stayed with him all the way and delivered a hard bodycheck that knocked him to the ice. I stopped, looked down at Harris, and said, "Y'know, Billy, you're not going to go around me anymore."

I've always had a special sympathy for Harris because, like myself, he was a young player who jumped from the Canadian junior ranks into the limelight of the NHL and faced a tremendous amount of pressure right from the start. More than that, he was the guy the Long Island fans looked to for production in that opening NHL season, which made things even more difficult for 20-year-old Billy.

When Billy and I became teammates I tried to help him as much as possible. I noticed one thing about his change in style. In the junior league he had had a great move: He'd come down the right wing and, when he approached the defense, fake to the inside, then move to the outside and *then* cut back to the inside once again, completely fooling the enemy defense. But when he got to the NHL, he seemed to lose confidence in that move and just kept going to the outside all the time. Finally, I took him aside and suggested he try the move that had worked so well in juniors. (The trick in the NHL is to expand your repertoire as much as possible to keep the defense guessing.)

My own problems with the limelight were soothed quite a bit by my junior coach, Bill Long. He never let me get too big-headed and he taught me what discipline was all about—although I confess I didn't always agree with his techniques. Long loved to levy fines for everything from coming late to practice to missing curfews.

He was especially tough about curfews. We were supposed to be in bed at 11 P.M. with no ifs, ands, or buts. To be sure that we obeyed, Bill would phone the house at 11 to see if we were there. I didn't particularly like the curfew, and my dodge was to stay home 'til 11 to take Long's call—and I'd be out of the house at ten after 11. Eventually Bill got wise to my trick. He phoned me at 11, I was out at 11:10, and he phoned back at 11:30. The first time he did that Mom covered up for me. "Denis is out getting a newspaper," she told Bill. But you could fool the coach just so long, and soon I was getting socked with $15 and $25 fines. And not only for curfew violation.

Once, playing an away game in Oshawa, Ontario, an industrial city not far from Toronto, I was rooming with Bunny Larocque, who later became the Montreal Canadiens' goalie. Bunny and I were in our room drinking beer the night before the game when who should walk in but the coach himself. He looked at us, looked at the beer, said, "That's 50 bucks apiece," and walked right out.

Long's idea of discipline meant strict observance of curfew, wearing shirt and tie on all road trips, and drinking only milk and water—no soda pop and no beer. Long was an English-speaking Canadian coaching a team almost half made up of French-Canadians. This could have been a difficult situation—and very nearly *did* become one.

Several of the French-Canadians on the team got the impression that Long didn't like Frenchmen as a result of a couple of episodes involving myself, Larocque, and Pierre Jarry, a French-Canadian forward.

Although I was only a teen-ager then, I couldn't have been more acutely aware of the "differences" between the French-speaking bloc and the English-speaking bloc in my native Canada. Minority status was an obvious fact of life for French-Canadians, in every conceivable way. We made less money. Our language was the "second" language of the country. We were ridiculed the way a black man might be taunted by a white American. Perhaps the names they called us weren't quite as vulgar as "nigger," but they sure carried a sting to them; "Pepsi," "Peasouper," and, worst of all, "Frog" were constantly used to taunt French-Canadians.

I had more than a vague idea of where it had started; the French had settled North America in the 16th century, when Jacques Cartier planted a cross on the Gaspé peninsula. And they had a rather elaborate community in Quebec when the English came along and challenged them for the territory. For the French, it all came to an end on Quebec City's Plains of Abraham when Wolfe defeated Montcalm. After that, the English took over and, until the 20th century, we were a large and localized minority—but a minority nonetheless.

Although life for the French-Canadian improved in the 1900s, our people still felt (with good reason) that we could never make it in big business, government, and finance the way the English could. But there was one common ground where we experienced equality, and that was on the ice. Unlike the black man, who had been deliberately barred from major-league baseball for decades, the French-Canadian had been a part of big-league hockey since the beginnings of the game. Skaters such as Edouard "Newsy" Lalonde, Georges Vezina, and Frank Boucher were among the greatest who ever laced up a pair of skates. In the forties and fifties the name of Maurice "The Rocket" Richard was the biggest in hockey.

In a sense, Rocket Richard meant as much to a French-Canadian as the Pope means to a Catholic. Every *Québeçois* worth his salt followed The Rocket and his team, *les Canadiens,* as if his life depended on it. In March 1955, when Richard was suspended from the Stanley Cup play-offs by NHL President Clarence Campbell, a full-scale riot erupted along Rue St. Catherine in Montreal. A lot of people believed that the rioting was as much a protest against the English in general as it was over the hockey suspension.

I wasn't even two years old when that happened, but I was to hear about it from my family and to read stories about the French-English problem in history books and magazines. The split was quite evident at the outbreak of World War II when the government tried to introduce conscription. It had overwhelming approval in English Canada but less than one-third support in the province of Quebec. French Canada was seething with resentment and showed it by this demonstration against conscription.

By the time I had begun to play junior hockey, the situation had changed quite a bit in favor of the French. Our rights, including the greater use of the French language, had begun to be recognized on many fronts. More important, a general movement (similar to the radical ones of the United States) had been launched by younger French-Canadians to gain equality for French Canada. While I didn't approve of the violent methods employed by the FLQ and other extremist groups, I couldn't help but be aware of the unbelievably strong feelings of my people.

It was under these conditions that Larocque, Jarry, and I bristled over what we thought was harassment from the English-Canadian, Long. The business came to a head one week in which we had a lapse in the schedule. There was a practice on Wednesday but no game until Friday. So when I walked into the dressing room that Wednesday I was really angry. Bill had called another curfew check on me that night, and I began bitching out loud, wondering whether any of the other guys had been checked on. The English guys all said they hadn't been phoned, but Bunny said he had gotten a call, and Jarry did, too.

That really pissed me off, so I asked for a meeting with the coach after practice. There I asked him why he was bugging the French-Canadians. "Listen," he said, "it's when I *don't* phone you that you have to start worrying. You're heading for the top, but if you want to make it, you'll have to learn to tow the mark. My job is to make sure that you do, whether you like it or not."

My gut feeling was that Bill was not anti-French, and I accepted his explanation. But all of this was really incidental to my growth and development as a hockey player. I respected his rule as leader of our team. I felt intuitively that he was doing what was best for my game. (Which is another way of saying he didn't stifle me when I was on the ice.)

Other junior hockey coaches such as Roger Neilson of the Peterborough Petes, who doubled as a school principal, kept a tight rein on their players. He'd program them to the point where he'd fine them if they were late for school or work, and he'd trade or cut the player who was fined often enough. I remember him saying once, "Organization is a better word. I think players want to see evidence of organization."

Neilson once brought his dog, Jacques, to practice to illustrate a point about forechecking. Neilson stood behind the net and positioned the dog in front. No matter how many times Neilson started to move, the dog stayed put, showing the players that even a dog had the patience to wait until his opponent made the first move.

I know that Neilson has been a winning coach, but I think his method of coaching youngsters has resulted in his programming more hockey players than anyone in junior coaching. The guys who come out of Peterborough are like skating robots. I remember an article about Neilson in the April 5, 1975, issue of *Weekend,* a Canadian magazine. The author, Chris Zelkovich, watched the Petes in action and met Neilson after the game. Neilson told Chris that it was the dullest game the Petes had played all year. "No," said Zelkovich. "It was no duller than most of them!"

Bill Long never programmed us, and as a result the 67s were never dull. In fact, we were so exciting that we outdrew the WHA team when they played in Ottawa and knocked them right out of the city and into Toronto. Once, though, I got a bit upset about a decision by Long that smelled of "programming." It happened during a game against the London Knights which got more and more brutal as it came down to the final minutes of the third period.

There had been so many fights in this particular game that most of the better players on both teams, including myself, had been tossed out and were watching from the sidelines. With two minutes left, we were leading, 4–3, and the one player on the Knights who could turn the game around for them was Darryl Sittler, later captain and superstar of the Toronto Maple Leafs. (During the 1975–76 season he scored six goals in a single game against the Boston Bruins.)

Forey leaped over the boards and moved to the face-off circle, opposite Sittler. The minute the puck was dropped, Forey dropped his gloves and started swinging. Sittler had no choice. He defended himself and swung back at Connie. (Oddly enough they were both good friends off the ice.)

Both players were tossed out with major penalties. With Sittler gone the Knights couldn't score, and we skated off with a 4–3 win. Whether or not this was "strategy," it served to emphasize a point that simply could not be avoided: Junior hockey, even if it is a game for teen-agers who are still supposedly amateurs, had become as intense as the NHL, and the desire to "win at all costs" was harbored by coaches up and down the line.

I felt this intensity very personally in the next few years because of two events in my hockey career: the departure of my big brother, Jean, to the pros—leaving me "alone" on a major team for the first time in my life—and an incident that will live with me for the rest of my life, the bout with Fran McKey.

# 5

## HIGH STICKS

When training camp opened for the Ottawa 67s in September 1969, I had an empty feeling in the pit of my stomach. For the first time in my hockey career brother Jean wasn't in Ottawa to give me physical support and guidance if I needed it. He had been signed by the NHL's Los Angeles Kings and farmed to their Springfield club of the American League. I knew it would never be the same with big brother gone, but I had prepared myself for the day this would happen. I had made "arrangements" a year earlier, when Jean still was at my side.

The turnabout occurred during a game with the Montreal Junior Canadiens, the flagship team of the NHL Canadiens' farm system. The Junior club was loaded at that time with such outstanding prospects as Richard Martin, Gil Perreault, and an exceptionally tough defenseman named André "Moose" Dupont, who later made a name for himself with the Philadelphia Flyers. Dupont was always among the leaders in penalty minutes, and he was generally feared as much for his temper as for his genuine toughness.

He failed to scare me the way I'm sure he put the fear of God into other young players. Our clash was inevitable. On this night we collided, our sticks instinctively went high, simultaneously creasing our respective chins, and a split second later the gloves were off and we were swinging freely.

I had landed a couple of good punches when, to my astonishment, someone grabbed Dupont from behind and pulled him away. Next I saw brother Jean chasing Dupont all over the rink like he was in a tag-team wrestling match. Jean caught Dupont and was belting him like a wild man when the fight was broken up by the officials.

Jean, naturally, was trying to be the good-guy big brother and, in retrospect, I appreciated it. But at that moment I was so embarrassed I felt like belting him. What he was doing—on my behalf—couldn't have been more damaging to my pride than if Dupont had scored a knockout over me. After the game I sat down with Jean over a couple of beers and laid it on the line, "Hey. Leave me alone. Let me fight my own battles." There were no hard feelings; Jean understood just as he had when I made the same request at other times. But I made up my mind that the next time out, during a game against Hamilton, I would put his non-intervention policy to a test.

On the day before the game I had been initiated to the traditional horror show for young players called "The Shave." It's a fairly disgusting practice, but one that has become commonplace in and out of the pros. Some NHL teams even carried an "official shaver," usually the oldest player on the team, whose job was to shave every piece of hair off the rookies—which meant pubic hair as well as chest hair and hair on top of the head. We were a bit more prudish on the 67s and, as a result, all they did was shave my head; the rest was considered sacred. Still, it proved very embarrassing the next night out.

I was prepared to get into a fight with somebody on the Hamilton club, just to see whether Jean would leave me alone. So, when I collided with one of the Hamilton players—I don't even remember who it was—I opened up a flurry of punches, with one eye on Jean to be sure he didn't intervene.

I was 15 and my opponent was a last-year man, which meant he had to be at least 19. I hit him well from the start and won the fight, but not exactly as I wanted to. Somewhere along the way my helmet fell off and my well-shaven head was exposed to the crowd. It was certainly one of the most embarrassing moments of my career. As soon as I realized what all the people were laughing at, I froze in my tracks and stopped slugging. Vanity had scored a TKO over Denis Potvin, the fighter.

Although I had already been in  number of battles, I had not even come close to developing a reputation as a fighter the way a Moose Dupont or a Dave Schultz had. But now that Jean was playing pro hockey I was on my own. And with the physique of a 26-year-old instead of a 16-year-old, I really began to feel my oats.

I learned that you had to play hard and tough. As far as I was concerned, there was no more beautiful sight in hockey than a good, hard, clean bodycheck. I soon found that I didn't feel right unless I flattened at least one player every game. I mean *really* lay them out. I discovered it was very important to me, psychologically. You wouldn't believe how effectively one hard hit can demoralize the opposition and lift your team. When a player sees his friend crawling off the ice, he's hurt, too.

Some people have said that nobody who plays organized hockey can be scared because once you get in a game, be it junior level or NHL, you have to be tough. There may be something to that, but on the other hand there are degrees of toughness on a hockey rink. The saying went something like this: All hockey players are tough but some hockey players are tougher than others. I could see that during a game when I was in a hitting mood. I could see guys on the opposition skating around with scared looks on their faces, wondering who'd be next, and it began to feel good, knowing that *I* was the guy scaring them.

I was 15 years old at the time, just a few weeks from turning 16. The date was October 2, 1969—I'll remember it till my dying day. We opened the season at home against a team from St. Catherines, Ontario, a city not very far down Lake Ontario from Toronto. St. Catherines was one of the hottest hockey teams in the league in those days. Its junior team had sent such first-rate players as Bobby Hull, Stan Mikita, and Elmer Vasko to the NHL and there was a feeling that hockey, on a different level of course, was as important to the people of St. Catherines as it was to the folks in Montreal and Toronto.

Perhaps that will help explain why Fran McKey, who was skating on the right wing for the St. Catherines Black Hawks, played the way he did that night. I was tempted to say he was exuberant, but McKey went beyond that. He was a rookie in the league, he was 16, a skinny kid almost 6′4″ tall, and he was obviously trying to make an impression before the Ottawa crowd. One writer had said McKey had "lots of promise and a sharp needle." All I knew was that he was mighty big standing next to me. When I looked at him, I wasn't staring at his face, I was looking straight at the Indian crest on his jersey.

I was to see a lot of that jersey as the game wore on. Normally I don't pay much attention to a particular member of the opposition, but McKey began needling me in the opening period and kept it up into the second.

"Hey, Potvin," he taunted, "why doncha get the coach to change yer diapers?"

His act really angered me. He hit our people left and right and took some unnecessary runs at Ottawa players that meant only one thing to me: He was spoiling for a fight. He took a run at me and I knew sooner or later I'd have to retaliate.

When one of the St. Catherines players shot the puck the length of the rink, it looked like "icing" would be called, which meant a face-off deep in the Black Hawks' end of the rink. Since I was the Ottawa defenseman nearest the puck, I raced back for it.

I must have been about a dozen feet from the puck when I heard the sound of skates behind me. Hockey players are trained—actually it's more a conditioned reflex—to keep their ears open for the crunch of skate against ice because it could mean a broken head administered by some skating madman about to ram you into the boards. It's a question of survival. When I detected McKey's rumbling behind me, I glanced back instinctively and saw this big guy coming at me. Sometimes it's possible to gird yourself for an impending collision. I tried to prepare myself for this one, for McKey clearly could demolish me with one check. But it was too late for me to get my bumper up. He ran me into the end boards. His stick was behind my legs. It was all I could do to avoid falling on my head. I was extremely tired at that point, much too knocked out to start anything then and there with McKey. But I filed his number in my mind.

A face-off had been called, so we all had to move to the other end of the rink. I pulled myself together and headed to the St. Catherines end. McKey continued the needling.

"Hey, Denis, where are yer diapers? Where's yer lollypop?"

That still didn't bother me; I'd heard it before and I knew I'd hear it again. But, this time I wanted it to stop.

Apparently McKey didn't intend to de-escalate the warfare. Quite the contrary; as soon as the puck was dropped at the face-off McKey hit one of our guys in the stomach, knocking him flat. When I saw that I went straight for McKey. As the "policeman" on our team, I had to restore order.

He saw me coming, lowered his stick in bayonet fashion, and speared me right in the stomach. That did it; I dropped my gloves, he dropped his, and the fight of my life was underway. Since McKey was so much taller than I, I had to avoid his long reach. Right off I hit him five or six times without getting anything of consequence in return. Because he was tall, I got in close and kept pounding him with both fists until he grabbed me in a desperate headlock to thwart my blows. His strategy worked for a second or two as he began belting me on top of my helmet.

When I felt the blows on my head, I grabbed him around the back of his legs, lifted him up, and threw him to the ice. (I learned later that the impact broke his collarbone.) McKey was down, and I went right after him, kneeling so I could look him square in the eyes. When he tried to lift his head, I hit him so hard his head hit the ice and he went out.

I was exhausted, but my fury still wasn't completely spent. As the referee grabbed me by the neck and pulled me away, I fell backwards to a point where my left skate-blade lifted directly over McKey's head. For that split second it crossed my mind that I could bring my sharp blade down, guillotine-style, over his head. Before I ever moved, the referee, no doubt sensing my intentions, grabbed my leg. Despite my anger at the time, I'm convinced that I would never have hit him with my skate. It was just a thought.

The results for McKey were dreadful. He had a fractured skull, a broken collarbone, and two black eyes. I had a pair of sore knuckles.

I was concerned about McKey. He was carried off the ice on a stretcher with a face that Ottawa columnist Ed MacCabe said "looked like a bag of golf balls." The attendants kept asking McKey who he was and, after a rather tense delay, he remembered. But he didn't know where he was and he kept asking. "We're still right by the ice," an attendant reassured him, "we're in Ottawa."

Considering the damage I had done to McKey, I was expecting retribution from someone on the St. Catherines club. It happened after the fight. A kid named Gary Cunningham seemed intent on crowning me with his stick. He skated around, pointing his stick at me, raising it in a menacing manner. Bill Long grabbed me by the shoulder. "Don't move!" he said. And in a second all the players on my team formed a circle around me to make sure nobody on the Black Hawks could pull a fast one.

Then a referee escorted me off the ice. I sensed a strange atmosphere in my own home rink: Instead of cheering, there was a heavy aura of ugliness. It was a stark kind of quiet, as if every one of the 10,000 fans knew what damage I had done, but I didn't.

"It was the worst beating I've ever seen a man get in hockey," Jack Gatecliff, sports editor of the *St. Catherines Standard,* said later. "McKey was never the same player after that."

For that matter, I wasn't the same either. I spent the rest of that season in a state of apprehension. Enemy players took shots at me and I accepted them because I kept thinking of the fight and how much of my pride had been lost in that moment.

Apart from the damage I had inflicted on McKey, I was disturbed by the manner in which I had lost control of myself. I had never before felt an overwhelming sense of fury like that, and it scared me; I had completely lost my senses in that brief flurry. And it took quite a bit of time before I could break my depression. Part of the "cure" was my ability to rationalize my actions. I said to myself, Hey, Denis, that guy McKey was spearing you and could easily have put *you* in the hospital the way you put him in. Once my rage had abated, I sort of felt myself again.

Unfortunately, the publicity that resulted from that fight caused a lot of trouble. St. Catherines coach Brian Shaw made a predictably big stink over the battle. "My kid got the hell beat out of him," said Shaw, "he was down and out . . . and Potvin was still pounding on him . . . and those linesmen were just standing around and watching. It was a badly handled game."

Two days after the fight I got a call from my brother, Jean, who was playing for the Springfield Kings. "Denis," he asked, "what the hell did you do to that McKey?" I asked him what he meant; all I did was get into a fight.

"Goddammit, we heard out here that you hit the guy over the head with your stick and gave him a concussion."

"Oh, no," I told him, "I never used the stick; you know that, Potsy! I'd never hit a guy on the head with my stick."

"Yeah," he reassured me, *"I* know it, but everybody's reading it differently and comin' over to me saying, 'Hey, Jean, what kind of animal is your brother, Denis?' I had some explainin' to do."

I knew it would take a lot of time before the emotional wounds healed. McKey was out of action for a couple of months before he returned. I saw him once before the season ended, but I hardly recognized him. He was wearing a helmet and appeared to have lost a lot of weight. It just didn't seem like the same Fran McKey. In a sense, I was glad to see the guy back in uniform; some people had warned me that he might never be able to play again. Once the game started we had very little contact with each other. I ran into him a couple of times—innocuous checks—but that was it. In fact, the only reaction came from some wise-guy fan in the stands. After I hit him the second check, the fan carped, "Why don't you try him again, McKey?"

It was easy for Ottawa fans to be cocky about the incident. In St. Catherines it was something else and, believe me, I was really worried the first time I skated in McKey's arena after the fight. I hoped that everything would have cooled down and the fans had forgotten about it. I remember sitting in the dressing room before the game, saying to the guys, a little scared-like, "Hey, gang, if anything happens out there, we're in this together, eh! Help me out."

I started on left defense and Pete Laframboise took the face-off and shoveled the puck back to me. Damn it if the puck didn't bump right over my stick and roll into the corner of the rink. My mind started reeling. Oh-oh, I thought, St. Catherines has its big guys on the ice. I turned around and skated toward the puck, the same way I did when McKey belted me to start the ruckus back in October. This time my heart was pounding twice as hard, and I was racing so I could wheel around before anyone was near me. It seemed like a lifetime. When I got to the puck I spun in my tracks, expecting a horde of Black Hawks to descend on me with their sticks in the "impale-him" position.

For a moment, I thought I saw a mirage: Instead of a flock of Black Hawks, there was nothing but clear ice between me and the blue line. It was the funniest thing—nobody had come after me. That was by far my most therapeutic moment since the McKey incident had taken place. It gave me renewed courage and seemed to wipe out all the mental roadblocks I had encountered. From that point on, I dominated the game, scored two goals and three assists, and we beat St. Catherines in their own building, 6–2.

How come they let me alone? My theory is that the Black Hawks, to a man, thought I was nuts after the way I had pummelled McKey. I figured that they didn't want to touch a "crazy man." And it was a theory I didn't want to discourage. I certainly wasn't going to go around and say to everybody, Hey, I'm Denis Potvin, Mister Nice Guy!

The media reacted in various ways. After the battle, the first reporter to see me in the dressing room was Eddie MacCabe, the Ottawa writer. I remember what he wrote the next day: "Denis Potvin was stripped and showered and standing there as solid as a tall oak stump . . ."

Clem Kealey of the *Ottawa Journal* said I had given "an outstanding lesson in the art of self-defense."

Some time later Earl McRae wrote an article about me in *The Canadian* and said: "Potvin has seldom been bothered since the fight. The enemy respects his hips and shoulders and they respect his fists."

McRae had spoken to McKey, and Fran's comments gave me an idea of his thinking: "I can't remember very much about it," he told McRae. "I know it happened around the blue line and I can remember thinking I didn't want to throw any punches because there'd be a fight and my nose might get hurt. I was already badly bruised and I didn't want it to get hurt again. Next thing I know I'm going down and that's all I remember. I woke up in the hospital.

"I was out about two months but I came back. The collarbone didn't mend properly and the next season I had a poor training camp and there was talk of trading me. I can't say how it (the beating) bothered me, it's hard to know these things."

I got a lot of grief as a result of the McKey bout, but I also have to admit that it gave me a certain notoriety which paid dividends in the long run. For better or worse, I had developed a "reputation." More and more stories were being printed about me—and toughness was a theme of many of them.

Once my confidence was restored during that return visit to St. Catherines, when the Black Hawks players in my end of the rink seemed to have evaporated, I developed into a total hockey player. McRae said it best about me when he wrote:

"It's obvious Potvin is something special. He's part of the play but then again he's not. He seems to transcend the action. His moves are so cool, so confident, never false. He seems to seethe with arrogance, disdain for all around him. He rules all he surveys and there is no one to threaten his kingdom. He seldom completes a game without leaving a legacy of human destruction."

At the age of 17 I had learned the meaning of the word "image," and I wasn't totally delighted with the direction in which I was going.

# 6

# AGENTS AND IMAGERY

I wasn't aware of it at the time, but the collective effect of all the newspaper and magazine stories about me was to fatten my ego to a point where I became unbearable to some of my friends and my family. One day a buddy approached me in high school and said simply, "Denis, you've changed." No more, no less.

That worried me. I knew exactly what he was talking about; I had gotten so cocky about my playing that it had affected some of my relationships with classmates. I didn't want it to be that way. I wanted my friends to treat me as an equal. I wanted to drink beer with them and shoot pool with them and not act above any of them. I realized I had to be Denis Potvin, the person, first and Denis Potvin, the hockey player, second. I tried very hard to stay low-key with my chums, but it wasn't so easy with my family.

I was a grown-up as far as the media was concerned, but I was still treated as a child by my parents. Unlike other junior hockey stars who moved away from their homes at age 14 or 15, I was still living with my parents beyond age 16 and feeling more and more uncomfortable about it. I wanted my independence, like so many young men my age, and my parents—especially Dad—were not exactly helping. I wanted to go my own way and Dad wouldn't let me.

He'd bug me about every little thing: "Denis, you didn't make your bed. Denis, you didn't play well last night. You didn't do this; you didn't do that." It reached a point where I couldn't do anything right in his eyes.

My reaction was to avoid him wherever possible. I'd make it my business to get up late enough in the morning so that he had already had breakfast and left for work. I'd make a point of missing supper and coming back home after 11 P.M. so that he was already asleep. I wanted it that way, and soon I'd gone weeks without seeing my dad. But that still wasn't enough as far as I was concerned.

What I really wanted was a complete break with the family, and I sought the proper time and place to pull off the move. The time finally came when my parents announced they were leaving for a weekend trip to Montreal to see Jean, who was playing for the Los Angeles Kings. I had a home game in Ottawa on Friday night, so it would have been impossible for me to get to Montreal even if I had wanted to.

Once they had left Ottawa, I sat down and wrote a long letter to my parents, explaining why I was leaving; how I was a big boy now; that I still loved them very much and that I hoped they wouldn't be too upset about my moving out. I put the letter on the kitchen table, went out and played my game for the 67s, then came home and packed my gear. Even though it was the middle of winter I packed my baseball glove. I wanted to take it with me because I was convinced that once I had left home, my father would never let me back in the house. I wasn't taking any chances. I took my glove, my clothes, everything. I packed them into my Impala and said bye-bye to the house.

My destination wasn't around the world but, more modestly, around the block. I had arranged to stay with a friend who lived by himself in a basement apartment nearby. He offered me a room with a telephone, and I set up house there in a semi-clandestine way. The only man who had my phone number was my coach, Bill Long. I told him what I had done and insisted that he not tell my dad.

It was a short but very wrenching experience for me because I had almost nobody to confide in except a friend who was a fireman and worked a night shift. If Jean had been around it would have been a lot easier for me.

I knew it would only be a matter of time before Dad caught up with me, and in a couple of weeks he had tracked me down. There was more than a little urgency in his pursuit because Mom had taken sick right after I left home and she had gone to the hospital. She was tortured by my decision to leave—she was "losing" her third and last son in a manner that displeased her greatly. Learning that she was hospitalized bothered me terribly because my move had backfired.

I felt frustrated because the person I was really rebelling against was my father, but he wasn't showing any pain. Meanwhile, my mother was in the hospital, torn to pieces by what I had done. It wasn't until quite a while later that I learned how deeply Dad himself had suffered from my abrupt departure.

When Dad finally learned my whereabouts and got in touch with me, he wasn't nearly as furious as I thought he would be. Quite the contrary, he invited me to dinner and we agreed to meet at a popular Ottawa restaurant, Al's Steak House. There we had our "reunion."

This was to be one of the most significant and poignant moments in my life. When Dad arrived I was uneasy, but he helped me relax. The two of us just sat across the table over beer and cigarettes—which were, in effect, symbols of my independence because, for the first time in my life, I was smoking *and* drinking beer in front of Dad, without reprisal or fear of reprisal. My father was an absolute prince about the entire episode.

We talked for some time. I presented my side of the case, my desire to be independent, my feeling grown-up already. I told him that all I wanted was some respect as I approached manhood. He gave me his side, his natural instinct as a father to want the best—or what he considered the best—for me. "You have a coach to teach you about hockey," he said, "and a father to bring you up."

After hashing things out into the night we finally shook hands. He told me the door of the house would always be open to me and, two weeks later, when I walked in, I found that he was right. As soon as I came back, my mother recovered and returned from the hospital.

I wish I could say that I had finally gotten myself out of the doghouse with my father, but there was one more episode after I returned home that stung him quite a bit. This was in my next-to-last year of junior hockey with the 67s, the 1971–72 season.

In January 1972 I injured my wrist in a game at St. Catherines. I was carrying the puck over the center red line and was about to shoot it into the corner of the rink when I was bodychecked. Just as the guy hit me I brought up my stick in self-defense and nudged him forward. My wrist bent back and popped.

I didn't want to quit in the middle of the game because otherwise I was feeling good and, sometimes, a hockey player feels better trying to shake off an injury by getting back into the game than by sitting on the sidelines. So I took my regular time on defense—and soon realized that I had no strength in my wrist at all. After the game I told the coach, and he had the doctor take a look at my wrist. The doctor said I had nothing more than a sprain, but I found that the wrist got weaker and weaker until it reached the point where I thought another doctor should look at it.

We saw a specialist who found I had a broken bone in the wrist and put it in a cast. But after a while I got restless and decided I'd try to play wearing the cast. I had heard stories about Dickie Moore of the Montreal Canadiens winning an NHL scoring championship in the late fifties while wearing a cast over a broken hand. But when I took the ice and started wheeling with the puck, I discovered that the cast on my wrist got soft and my wrist began moving—as it should not have been moving under the circumstances—and the doctor ordered me off the skates when he heard about it. "The wrist," he said, "has to be completely immobilized."

Well, that meant I was through as a player for the season, and believe me it was a terrible downer. Here I was at the top of my junior game, the 67s were trying for the Memorial Cup (junior hockey's answer to the Stanley Cup), and I was ruled inactive. It got me so terribly depressed that finally one of my non-hockey-playing buddies began worrying about me and suggested a temporary change of scenery: Acapulco, Mexico.

My pal came up with a cheap package deal—$219 for a week in the sun. I said, Let's go. In a couple of weeks I would regret those words.

As Earl McRae put it, "His team was in the finals and everybody felt he was sort of a quitter, a deserter."

I knew nothing of this. I had a pleasant time in Mexico, unwound completely, climbed out of my depression, and returned on a real upbeat—until I stepped inside my house. There was my father, as livid as I had ever seen him, holding a bundle of newspapers, all with articles about how Denis Potvin had left his team while it was getting knocked out of the playoffs. I could see from the stories that everyone was getting on my ass over my trip, each of them making the same point: I should have stayed with the team.

It made me think about my image and my reputation. I never felt I had done the wrong thing. I was so down mentally at the time I had to get away. I just couldn't have stayed in Ottawa another week. Fortunately, some people stuck up for me. One of them was a guy named Dave Schatia.

"Really," Schatia said a year later, "it wasn't Denis' intention to desert the 67s. Not at all. He felt really down and discouraged that he couldn't play." Schatia had good reason for sticking up for me; he was to become my agent. Almost overnight, I-M-A-G-E became all-important.

Compared with such sophisticated sports as baseball and football, hockey was still in the Middle Ages when it came to the care, feeding, and, most of all, the paying of its players. Owners realized that most players echoed the sentiments of the immortal Rocket Richard, who once had said, "I played hockey because I loved it. Anything I got paid was considered a bonus."

When the NHL was still a six-team league, an attempt to develop a players union was promoted by such first-rate skaters as Doug Harvey, Ted Lindsay, and Tod Sloan. But the owners, sensing a rebellion, quashed the union plans and punished Harvey and Lindsay by trading them to New York and Chicago, respectively, from Montreal and Detroit (which were considered more desirable teams to play with at the time).

"If you fought the owners," said Bob Pulford, when he was centering for the Toronto Maple Leafs, "you could be sent to the minors forever."

But expansion and Bobby Orr changed everything. When Orr signed a two-year contract with the Bruins in September 1966 he was accompanied by a man who was to turn the entire hockey world upside-down, attorney R. Alan Eagleson, affectionately known to the players as "The Eagle."

Eagleson was a Toronto lawyer who had been asked by Doug Orr, Bobby's dad, to handle his son's negotiations with Bruins manager Hap Emms. Emms didn't want Eagleson around—at the time NHL managers wouldn't even hear of an agent entering their inner sanctum—but Hap had no choice. The Bruins, then a pretty bad team, were desperate for a star like Orr, and Emms relented. Eagleson got a tremendous amount of ink over that coup, and suddenly all the hockey players were whispering his name in awe. Then, in December 1966, he scored another major victory when he was asked to represent the *entire* Springfield Indians American League team in a battle they were having with the club owner, Eddie Shore. The Eagle brought Shore to his knees. And now he was ready for bigger and better action.

The Boston Bruins were so impressed with the way Eagleson had defeated Shore that they figured maybe, just maybe, he could take on the NHL owners. They asked The Eagle to organize an NHL Players' Association, and he agreed. By May 1967 all but two NHL players had signed with the NHL Players' Association, and a month later the NHL governors recognized the group.

With that a new era dawned for hockey players. Their salaries, which had been somewhere in the subterranean depths, climbed to the stratosphere. A player like Vic Hadfield, for example, earned only $8,000 a year before the Union was formed but climbed to $175,000 after expansion and the Union. Eagleson's success spawned a whole new industry: the hockey agent. By 1972, when the World Hockey Association had arrived, it seemed that there were as many agents as players.

I was bombarded with calls from these guys as soon as I had made a name for myself with the 67s. With the NHL already into its second big expansion and a third—in Long Island and Atlanta—on the way, the agents and lawyers knew there was money to be made for hockey players (and themselves).

You wouldn't believe how they came out of the woodwork! Some would come up to me after a game in Ottawa and say, "Hey, I'm just out of college and I'd like to represent you in contract talks with the NHL." Still others would phone me at home. But one team of lawyers was distinctly different from the horde that besieged me for so many months. They were David Schatia and Larry Sazant of the Montreal law firm of Schatia, Sazant and Levine.

Schatia and Sazant were impressive in every way. Wearing very modish three-piece suits, they *looked* good. They seemed to know what they were doing. They had all the necessary legal savvy. They knew the game and they appeared to have all the right answers to my questions. Besides, they complimented me on my playing and, of course, that made me feel good. So we agreed to a rendezvous at the R&R Restaurant in Ottawa.

When we met they had with them a little contract; they seemed to have all the right papers at the right time. But I told them they'd have to talk to my father before I signed anything. And the minute Dad saw the contract he looked it over with a fine-toothed comb and began picking it apart, line by line. "We'll change this," he told me, "and we'll change that. Y'know, Denis, this is the same contract they give to every Goddamned Joe in Canada. You're going to be the best, so you're not going by any of these rules."

I met with Schatia and Sazant again, told them what my father had proposed, and we altered the contract in my favor. After a few more discussions, I decided they were for me. They also represented Rick Martin and René Robert of the Buffalo Sabres and Rick Kehoe of the Toronto Maple Leafs, so I figured I was in pretty good company.

Just before I agreed to sign with Schatia and Sazant I was almost intercepted by The Eagle himself. Eagleson had become the most famous and most successful hockey attorney in Canada by now, and the fact that *he* got in touch with *me* was an honor. I asked him if I could bring my father along and he readily agreed, so we met for dinner at the Skyline Hotel in Ottawa.

We talked over a steak dinner—I had two steaks that night and I'm not sure why I remember that so vividly—and we seemed to enjoy each other's company. The Eagle is a dynamic guy who looks like a little quarterback who's always moving or talking. I was impressed with him *as a person*. He was loose and amusing—quite a contrast to Schatia and Sazant—and he wasted no time giving me his pitch, which went like this: "Hey. You either go with me, or you don't go with me. If you go with me, you'll have a good time, a lot of fun."

That sounded like a nice parlay. In fact it sounded so good to my father that, when we got home that night, he said I should sign with The Eagle. But I shook my head no.

Dad couldn't believe it until I explained that I had done a little research on my own. I had learned that Eagleson had 27 other lawyers working under him and those were the guys who handled his hockey players—with the exception of Bobby Orr. "Look," I told Dad, "The Eagle is a great guy and all that, but I want somebody who will work hard for me, and do for me what Eagleson does for Orr." I felt he would pay much too much attention to Orr's business to suit me and, in the long run, it would hurt my interests.

It wasn't an easy decision. Before I finally signed with Schatia and Sazant I told Eagleson exactly how I felt. He said, "Don't worry, Denis, we can work that out. No problem. Orr has one way of doing things, and you have another." He was very persuasive, but I had developed an independence by now that wasn't easily swayed. Thanks, I told him, but no thanks!

I was a bit sorry when I did that. The more I thought about it, the more incredible it seemed that Denis Potvin, still a junior hockey player, had turned down Alan Eagleson. But I stuck to my decision and I signed with the Montreal lawyers before my last season with the 67s.

My friends couldn't believe their ears when I told them what I'd done. Bypass Eagleson? Are you crazy? How could you?

"Eagleson is a politician and an attorney," I explained, "and he's head of the players' union. He's got too many things going for him—too many things to do. If I go with him, I'll end up his pupil instead of his boss. When I hire an agent I'm supposed to tell him what to do."

So I went with Schatia and Sazant and waited to see what they could do for Denis Potvin. I was in a pretty good bargaining position by now. The WHA had survived its first season and was apparently going into its second year of operation, 1973–74, in better shape than it had been in its first. The NHL was now a 16-team league. The Islanders and Flames were completing their first year of operation and both teams were drawing well. Schatia was in touch with a lot of teams and sort of emerged as spokesman for me. He began telling the media which teams were after me and what he thought of my prospects.

Three WHA teams, the New York Raiders, the Chicago Cougars, and the Ottawa Nationals had made offers, but Schatia was waiting to hear from the NHL, where the real money was (not to mention the prestige). Writers began pestering Schatia for estimates of the contract offers I was receiving. One day I read his reply in the newspaper:

"The figures are very harmful to a player. Assume somebody said Denis Potvin was worth half-a-million dollars and he goes into that dressing room and hasn't been producing for the first few weeks. The other guys will be down on him. It's tough enough adjusting from an amateur to a professional and having all that responsibility heaped upon your shoulders without having the guys feel here's a big bonus baby who can't do a damn thing."

Somebody asked Schatia if I would be the highest paid rookie in pro hockey. "We'd be derelict in our duties," he told the guy, "if we didn't accomplish something along those lines."

My agents had a good basis of comparison. The number one NHL draft pick in 1972 was Billy Harris, who had played against me for the Toronto Marlboros. He was chosen by the Islanders and, according to the newspaper reports, he was getting $150,000 a year over two years as "the highest paid rookie in NHL history."

I wasn't sure whether I would top Harris or not, though I did know there was an awfully good chance I'd wind up skating alongside Harris on the Islanders. They were having an awful first year in 1972–73, and consequently they would have the first pick in the 1973 junior draft. That meant they would have first chance to pick me.

"It looks," said an article in *The Canadian,* "as if the Islanders will get him." The article also mentioned Schatia prominently: "Grooming Potvin for future fame and fortune takes up most of Schatia's time. Image is the big thing."

Here I was, still a teen-ager, and I was being "image-inized." Schatia didn't mince any words about it. "When a person has the makings of a superstar such as Denis we have to be very very careful about protecting his image and his attitude.

"We're rebuilding his image this year, working very hard getting him psychologically attuned to what he can expect. Basically, our objective is to say, look, you're number one, you've got to play as if you're number one, you've got to establish in everyone's mind without a doubt that you are number one. Second, you've got to show everybody you are a *team* man, that you have qualities of leadership and winning for the team is the important thing. We've decided how he should handle himself on and off the ice, how to behave. He's matured a lot in the last year. He used to be a little more concerned with himself rather than those around him. He's coming along nicely. We're very pleased."

I wasn't.

When I read some of Schatia's quotes in *The Canadian* I got angry—especially with his remark, "He used to be a little more concerned with himself rather than those around him . . ." If anyone was going to build up Denis Potvin it was going to be Denis Potvin, not David Schatia and not Larry Sazant.

In our face-to-face dealings, Schatia and Sazant laid things out for me—they expected me to grasp everything but I couldn't. I was 19. It was impossible.

They asked me to check out with them every writer who called me for an interview before I talked. They wanted to approve the stories.

Schatia made me worry so about stories that I soon felt uncomfortable even talking to people. Imagine me telling a writer, "Hey, before you write that story, can I talk to my agent so we can check you out?"

Every little move I made was magnified into a big deal as the "image" was molded. If someone came up to me in a bar, I felt as if I had to push the beer aside. After all, Denis Potvin shouldn't be seen drinking beer, right? So image-makers thought. I began to feel guilty every time I puffed on a cigarette.

What's going on? I asked myself. I smoke. I drink beer. I've got nothing to hide.

There was, however, one thing I wanted very much to hide—and hide from: those headlines that linked me with another hockey player of repute, one Robert Gordon Orr.

# 7

# "HE'S ANOTHER BOBBY ORR"—UGH!

In 1967 Harry Howell of the New York Rangers won the James Norris Memorial Trophy, an award the NHL gives annually to "the defense player who demonstrates throughout the season the greatest all-around ability in that position." When Howell accepted the prize at the NHL convention that June he said something prophetic:

"I'm delighted to get the Norris Trophy because in the next ten years I think the award is going to be owned by one man—and that man isn't me."

Howell was talking about Bobby Orr, who was about to become the most talked about hockey player in the world. By 1973, before I made my professional debut, Orr had won the Norris Trophy six straight years and had been five times the NHL's most valuable player and twice its leading scorer. "In all my NHL years," said Hall of Famer Milt Schmidt, "Orr is the greatest player I have ever seen in the past, the greatest player at present, and if anyone greater should show up, I just hope the Good Lord has me around here to see him."

That's why I was disturbed, in my final year of junior hockey with Ottawa, to read the headlines in both English and French papers about me and my future in the NHL:

67S' POTVIN TOUTED AS NEXT BOBBY ORR
—*The Montreal Star*

DENIS POTVIN, LE PROCHAIN BOBBY ORR DE LA NATIONALE?
—*Le Droit,* Ottawa

67S' DENIS POTVIN TOUTED AS NEXT ORR
—*The Ottawa Journal*

ANOTHER BOBBY ORR? 67S' DENIS POTVIN PRAISED BY NHL VETS
—*The Ottawa Citizen*

ANOTHER BOBBY ORR IN THE MAKING . . . DENIS POTVIN STARS
WITH OTTAWA

*—The Hockey News*

In time, a reporter put the question to me. "Does it bother you, everybody saying you're another Orr?"

I answered as plainly and honestly as possible, "Yes, it does. There's Bobby Orr and there's me, Denis Potvin. Orr does things I don't do, and I do things he doesn't do. You can't compare us. I don't want everybody measuring me against Orr."

Fat chance. The newspaperman who asked me that question then wrote: "Best defenseman in junior hockey since Orr. Bigger than Orr. Stronger than Orr. Tougher than Orr. Meaner than Orr. Maybe even smarter than Orr . . ."

That's what I was up against—that and my feeling that I should have been in the NHL by this time. But the NHL had a rule that juniors were not eligible for the big league until the age of 20. I found it more and more difficult to psych myself up for a game. The challenge had gone out of competing with juniors. I knew that I could pretty much do what I wanted to do out there. But I also knew that I couldn't afford to let up because of those comparisons with Orr—and because I finally met *The Man* himself and was very impressed with Bobby, the person.

We met at a golf tournament just outside Montreal. I was there because my brother Jean, then in the NHL, was competing in the tourney. I had seen Orr around the course but made a point not to say a word to him. In truth, I was awed by the sight of Bobby and was too modest and embarrassed to strike up a conversation with him.

After the day's golf the guys got together in the clubhouse for drinks and gabbing. By this time I had gotten my nerve and, when I saw Orr standing at the other side of the room, I walked over to him and introduced myself. He was extremely cordial, much more so than I would have expected from a man in his position with a lot of his cronies around demanding his time. We talked for a while and then went our separate ways—until the affair ended, when a surprising and delightful thing happened.

As I headed for my car, Orr came up to me and asked, "Hey, Denis, whereya goin'?"

I told him I was heading home.

"Where's home?" he asked.

"Ottawa."

"How far from here?"

"About 120 miles. I'll be home by three in the morning."

"Man, that's crazy!" he said. "Why don't you come along with us?"

The "us" included Derek Sanderson and other stars I had heard of but had never met. It was an offer I couldn't refuse.

So I went with them to Montreal for some serious "nightclubbing" at Harlow's—one drink—and closed the joint. I said good night to Bobby and told him I really had to get going home. "Nah," he shot back, "come over to my hotel. I'll put you up for the night."

I couldn't believe my ears. Bobby Orr, Superstar, inviting *me* to his room. "No," I said, "I don't want to impose."

"It's nothing at all," Bobby insisted.

"Well, if it's okay with you, then it's okay with me."

So we drove to the Bonaventure, a beautiful new hotel in Montreal. Orr had a big room with two huge double beds. It was funny; Orr had a bunch of luggage there, and I walked in with a tiny shaving kit.

By now Bobby and I had developed a rapport that I wouldn't have believed possible. He was amazingly down-to-earth, one of the most regular people you could imagine, with absolutely no pretensions whatever. We talked until the dawn broke, about hockey and the problems I faced coming up to the NHL.

"I've heard a lot about you," he said, "although I've never actually seen you play. But I think I know what you're going through, because I went through the same thing myself: the pressure, the press clippings, the magazine articles. The important thing to remember, no matter how far you go, is to *be yourself!* On the ice and off. Play the game the best way you know how and don't let anyone tell you what to do. Be confident."

That moment will always be vivid in my mind. I had listened to every word Bobby said. After breakfast we said our good-byes and went our separate ways, he to his home in Parry Sound, Ontario, and I to Ottawa. I, Denis Potvin, had met and been hosted by The Greatest.

Still, as I tooled my car back to Ottawa, I knew more than ever that there's Bobby Orr and there's me; and we'll never be the same.

My final year of junior hockey should have been a breeze. It was my fifth winter in the Ontario Hockey Association's A Division and I knew the inside of each rink like I knew the blade on my stick. I was afraid of nobody, neither player nor team, and I was the center of attention, thanks to the press, the emergence of the World Hockey Association, and the competition for my talents. I was lucky that I hadn't been allowed to turn pro before the WHA forced the prices "way up." If I had gone to the NHL at 18, I would have had to take what they wanted to give me, because the WHA wasn't around then to convert hockey into a players'—rather than an owners'—market.

Another plus was my new coach in Ottawa. Bill Long, who had guided me for so many years, was a fine man; I appreciated all that he had done for me. But by now I felt I had outgrown him and his methods. Bill's disciplinary tactics, his fines, and what I saw as his lack of involvement with the players during practices began to annoy me. There was increasing talk about Long leaving Ottawa to take a coaching job in London, Ontario, and it happened at the start of the 1972–73 season. The club announced that Leo Boivin would replace Long behind our bench. This was fine; I had known Boivin for years and, before that, had heard about his defense work with the Boston Bruins and the Toronto Maple Leafs. Boivin was a short, stocky man with a heavy beard who had a reputation as one of the most devastating bodycheckers in the league. Because he was smaller than usual, he had a lower center of gravity and had developed a knack of moving in on an opponent and swinging his hips on impact. When that happened, the guy went flying.

Boivin used to teach at the Eastern Ontario Hockey School during the summer, and I spent some time there taking care of the kids who attended the school, making sure they got to the rink on time and doing general supervisory work. Working with Leo was a pleasure; I knew that playing for him would be a lot of fun, too. Boivin was more relaxed than Long and closer to the players. During practices, Leo would skate with us and shoot with us, being right in among the players. Bill could never do that because of his age; he'd just stand at one end of the rink and blow his whistle.

One of the questions in my mind was what Leo could do to improve my play. There was just so much a coach could do with a 19-year-old, but he did work a lot on my bodychecking technique—something at which he was expert. Day after day, he'd take me aside during practice and show me how to move in on an enemy skater.

Since I was considerably taller than Leo, I couldn't deliver a body-check in precisely the same manner he did. I couldn't bend down as low when I blasted someone with my hip, so I added another dimension, got more knee into the contact, and tried to catch the entire side of the opponent's leg, causing him to fall. I was enjoying hitting more than ever, but I wasn't totally satisfied with my own play. In fact, at a time when I should have been at the very top of my game, I began tailing off. It was almost like the bad joke about the kid who was "losing his legs" at age 19. No, I wasn't losing my legs; it was more a case of losing my concentration.

I considered myself the best player in the league, yet I found myself losing my concentration during games, and that was bad. I don't mean to belittle the opposition I had, but junior hockey just wasn't bringing out the best in me anymore. I was continually facing situations I knew I could handle, and this hurt me. One game in particular was a horror story.

It took place at Maple Leaf Gardens in Toronto against the Toronto Marlboros. This was a very important game for me because there were more scouts at the contest than had been at any other game in which I had played. Jim Proudfoot, sports editor of *The Toronto Star,* later wrote, "There were more elbowing infractions (among the scouts) around the coffee urn than there were out on the rink."

That was funny. What followed, however, stung me badly: "All of them might as well have stayed home. Aside from the free food, it was a wasted afternoon for them."

Proudfoot was right. The Marlboros won their game easily. It was embarrassing. The limelight was stolen by a 17-year-old left wing, Mark Howe, son of the Superman himself, Gordie Howe. I was well aware of the scouts, especially Earl Ingarfield of the Islanders, as well as a busload of fans who came down from Ottawa. We really laid an egg for them. Our club couldn't put it together, couldn't play as a team. I felt guilty since I was the oldest veteran on the club, and I felt an obligation to do something about it.

A lot of people have wondered why I played so poorly that night. The untold story is that our entire team was psyched out long before game time, but *not* by the opposition.

I was sitting in my room in the Westbury Hotel the day of the game when I heard a loud noise out on the balcony. I turned and saw a large, white object flash past the window. I ran to the balcony, looked down, and saw the blood-splattered body below.

When the team left the hotel for the pre-game dinner, we saw that the dead body had still not been removed by the police or an ambulance. It was the most sickening and scary thing I had ever seen in my life, and it completely distracted me from the game that night at Maple Leaf Gardens. I still get goose pimples when I think about it.

On the other hand, the tragic game had its sweet side. It demonstrated that I wasn't perfect, that I still made mistakes in every game, and that I had work to do before I turned pro.

That day wasn't very far off. The Islanders were destined to finish with the worst record in the NHL and thus to have first pick in the draft. Normally there wouldn't have been any guarantee that they'd go for me, but something happened late in the 1972–73 season that permanently altered my life. On March 5, 1973, the Islanders announced that they had traded veteran forward Terry Crisp to the Philadelphia Flyers for none other than my brother Jean.

It could have been just a coincidence that the Islanders selected Jean. He had established his credentials as a first-rate NHL defenseman and would have been an asset to any team. But some of us suspected that Islanders manager Bill Torrey hoped to pair Jean and me on the 1973–74 club. Meanwhile, the WHA teams were still on my trail. I told reporters that I would go where I could get the most for my talents, even though in my heart I was hoping for the NHL, and specifically Jean and the Islanders.

In the meantime, I had to concentrate on my final season and improve my game wherever possible. Coming up was the most significant game of my entire year—not a regularly scheduled contest, but an exhibition game against Russia's national hockey team, at Treasure Island Gardens in London, Ontario. I was one of eight OHA players invited to bolster the London Knights in their game with the Soviets. Just getting the invitation was a tremendous thrill—and I damn near blew it altogether, for want of a gallon of gasoline.

My first mistake was deciding to drive to London from Ottawa with Ian Turnbull, Blake Dunlop, Paul Sheard, and David Lee instead of taking the bus or the train. (We drove out in a Chrysler Imperial with a chap named Howard Darwin who was the owner of the 67s.) Usually the drive takes seven hours; if we left at nine in the morning, we should have been at the rink, comfortably, by four in the afternoon.

We were all so excited about the game that none of us paid much attention to the fuel gauge as it fell toward the left side of the "E." All of a sudden the car began lurching, coughing, sneezing, and at last stopping altogether. "Guess what," said Howard, "I think we're in trouble."

Trouble meant we were out of gas and stranded some 40 miles from London. I wasn't as worried about not getting to the rink by game time as I was that I'd miss my traditional afternoon pre-game nap and be in lousy shape for what looked like the most important game of my career.

We hiked for gas—I mean *hiked*—and lugged it back to the Imperial, and we drove into London after six in the evening. My hopes for a nap were shot. We hustled to a restaurant, ate a quick dinner, and went on to Treasure Island Gardens. I fully expected the game to be a disaster for me, just as the trip had been so far.

In the dressing room I felt kind of strange. There on the benches were fellows I had been hitting pretty hard over a period of four or five seasons: players such as Bob Gainey of Peterborough, Larry Goodenough and Dennis Maruk of London. Personal animosities are forgotten in moments such as these; we were united in our determination to whip the Russians.

We couldn't have been more keyed up, remembering how the Russians had embarrassed Team Canada in the well-publicized eight-game series in September 1972. Since then the Soviet hockey players had taken on the aspects of supermen. Their skating was supposed to be faster than anything seen on this continent. Their passing had already become legendary, and their devotion to the game was a throwback to the early days of hockey in North America. That was the word we had received. And so we were very anxious to prove that, even if we didn't win, we could give these fellows a run for their money.

I don't remember being so nervous before a game. My body was a bundle of knots that could only be unwound by physical contact. I made up my mind that as soon as the puck was dropped I would get *into* the game as quickly as possible. And the only way to do that would be to throw my weight around. When the puck was dropped, those Soviets started coming over our blue line in waves. And I stood there bouncing every red-shirted puck-carrier in sight. In the first period alone I think I hit 12 of them, more than I usually hit in an entire game.

I was amazed at myself; these Russians were big, strong men experienced in international competition. But I quickly realized that what they presented was a challenge that was bringing out the best in Denis Potvin. In fact, they had me playing *over* my head.

Their offensive strategy was obvious, and it played into my hands: The Soviet defensemen started a play by going behind their net. There they'd look for any one of three forwards who wheeled back and forth at center ice, waiting for the long pass. I could sense the pass, and I spent the night cutting across and stopping it before it reached their skaters.

By the second period they had been neutralized; it was then I realized that we actually had a chance to beat the Russians.

The Soviets tried a number of plays but we seemed to be able to stop each one. One play featured a forward carrying the puck into our zone and stopping dead in his tracks. He'd look from side to side for a free teammate but, by the time he found one, we had run him over and taken the puck away.

Occasionally a Soviet player would break through our defenses, but we had stayed even with them when the third period began. This would be our supreme test; we knew the Russians had tremendous stamina and, as the last period progressed, I realized that they were stronger than anybody I had ever played against. (Their strength was especially noticeable around the arms and upper body.)

Once I carried the puck into their zone and camped in front of the net, awaiting a pass. Then we lost the puck and I started in the other direction. But one of the Russian defensemen closed his legs around my stick. His legs had the power of a vise and it took me several seconds to yank my stick free. I was so angry, so frustrated—it was that hyper a game—that I pulled back my right arm and punched him in the jaw. He fell back and landed on his *derrière*. But he was back on his skates in no time at all, and he chased me up the ice, gesturing and shouting. His Russian sounded like "grunt, grunt, grunt" to me, and I remember thinking to myself, Who are these animals?

The Russians not only grunted, they *smelled* quite different from the average Canadian player. It was the smell of a skater whose equipment hadn't been cleaned for several weeks—very potent, very unpleasant. Even so, the Russians failed to overwhelm us. When the final buzzer had sounded, lo and behold, our motley collection of OHA juniors had beaten the Moscow Selects, 6–3. I scored a goal, Bob Gainey had two, and Ian Turnbull, John Held, and Dennis Maruk had each scored for us. Alexander Golikov, Vyacheslav Solodukhin, and Sergey Kapustin got the Russian goals.

It was a tremendous game for me. A day later, Frank Orr of *The Toronto Star* confirmed what I felt: "The poise and skill which Potvin displayed impressed the large number of NHL scouts on hand. They knew what he could do against boys, but wanted to see him against men. He didn't disappoint them."

Now the big question in my mind centered on the NHL draft in June 1973 and what the Islanders would do about me. As things turned out, it was all very positive. Schatia knew that I wasn't interested in the

WHA, and Roy Boe, the Islanders' president, had already gone on record saying that money would not be an object when it came to luring me to New York.

If the Russian game hadn't been enough to convince me that I was ready for the big time, the statistics helped. I concluded my last year in Ottawa with 35 goals and 88 assists, for a total of 123 points in 61 games. Better still, *I had broken Bobby Orr's junior hockey scoring record by 29 points.*

The 1973 junior draft was held in Montreal at the Queen Elizabeth Hotel. There were 150 junior players for the NHL teams to choose from. I thought that if I were going to be the number one pick, I ought to look like a special person. When I dressed for the occasion, I made a point of looking different; I wanted to look like anything but a hockey player. I wore a dark, pin-striped suit with a white shirt and a dark tie.

It was a smart decision. When I got to the hotel, I saw that the other players were all wearing flashy bow ties, checkered plaid suits with plaid pants—real hockey player-type stuff. "You look more like a business-man than a hockey player," one of the writers said. That made me feel very good. What made me feel not so good was a rumor going around that I might *not* become an Islander after all. I had heard from Schatia that the Canadiens were trying to swing a last-minute deal with the Islanders so that they could sign me to play for Montreal.

I know that every red-blooded French-Canadian is supposed to want to play hockey for *les Canadiens.* Still, I wasn't one of them. I didn't want to be traded to Montreal because I was afraid I'd be under tremendous pressure to be an instant superstar—and I knew there was a long list of players who had cracked under the strain of having to live up to those demanding Montreal rooters. I saw what had happened to Guy Lafleur in his rookie year, how they nearly drove him crazy, wanting him to be another Jean Beliveau, and I was anxious that nothing would come of the deal.

The rumors persisted. Schatia said that Sammy Pollock, the Cana-diens' manager, had offered the Islanders four good players for me.

Dad, Jean, and Debbie (then my girlfriend) were sitting behind the Islanders' table in the huge room where the draft took place. The proceedings began when Clarence Campbell, the elderly, distinguished-looking NHL president, walked to the dais and called for order.

"We are ready to begin," said Campbell, and the audience fell silent. The time had come for the team with the worst record in the previous season to make the first selection. The Islanders, who had 347 goals scored against them and who had finished at the bottom of the NHL, had the choice. Their manager, Bill Torrey, was a husky, affable fellow with long jowls and a penchant for wearing bow ties. Torrey was about to announce his choice when Sammy Pollock unexpectedly raised his hand. I thought my Adam's apple would sink right down to my toes.

"Mister Campbell," said Pollock in very businesslike fashion, "may I interrupt for a moment to have a word with Mister Torrey?"

Campbell nodded approval and it appeared my worst fears were about to be confirmed: Pollock was going to conclude the big deal. I'd be a Montreal Canadien in a matter of minutes.

Pollock, who had been sitting at the Canadiens' table at the other end of the room, very dramatically rose to his feet and walked across the room to Torrey. While hundreds watched, they spoke for a half minute that seemed like six months to me. I could see their lips moving, but I couldn't quite read them. I was certain they had made the trade. Finally, Pollock walked back to his seat and Campbell returned to the microphone.

"Bill Torrey of the New York Islanders, you have the first choice."

Torrey got to his feet, stuck out his chin, and, in the longest split second of my life, said, "The New York Islanders wish to draft as their first choice—Denis Potvin."

I swallowed hard, then turned to face a dozen people who seemed about to attack me: the radio, television, and newspaper people who wanted the "story." It was a marvelous moment for me—but I was acutely aware that it wasn't as sweet for another fellow my age who had skated alongside me for a number of seasons. That was Ian Turnbull, a big, strong defenseman who had once played against me on the Montreal Junior Canadiens and then become a teammate of mine on the 67s.

Turnbull and I were rivals when he played for the Junior Canadiens. At one point the newspapers tried to create a "feud" between us over whether Potvin or Turnbull was the best defenseman in the juniors. For a while I actually believed that he was better than I; then he was traded to Ottawa and we became pretty good friends, if still rivals in a sense.

One day, sitting at a restaurant in Peterborough, Ontario, just Ian and me, he said, "Y'know, Denny, it's going to be either you or me for number one junior defenseman in Canada."

I didn't say a word, but, from then on I felt a tremendous need to outplay Turnbull; I worked hard at it. It paid off when I became the number one pick. Turnbull wasn't picked until 15th.

But here I was, both French- and English-speaking reporters surrounding me, feeling so good, I wanted to spend the rest of the day and night answering their questions.

It was quite a scene. Here I was in one corner, babbling away. My father was running all over the place saying, "Hey, I'm Mister Potvin!" Jean was crying for joy because we were together again. And my mother, God bless her, handled the furor best of all—with a drink.

So my first meeting with the media was a huge success. Apparently they had expected me to limit my responses to short sentences and to make a hasty exit. No way. I was having so much fun I went on for five hours in French and English. I was prepared even for the inevitable "How do you compare yourself with Bobby Orr?"—and I fielded the question immediately.

"Being compared with Orr is nice," I told them, "but it's going to put pressure on me in my first year with the Islanders. I know I can cope with it. I hope the fans in New York can appreciate that playing in the NHL will be a whole new thing for me."

In those days I wore a Fu Manchu mustache, and for some reason the reporters made a big deal about that. One reporter wrote, "He is confident but not cocky." I liked that. I also liked the fact that they gave Jean a lot of attention. Hugh Delano of *The New York Post* asked Jean about me.

"Right now," said Jean, "he handles the puck as well as Brad Park or J. C. Tremblay. He's extremely strong, has what you call a booming slap shot, a wrist shot with quick release and he is a great skater. The thing he does best is hit. Boy, when he hits you, you feel it, I know. Denis can intimidate people."

That's all the writers had to hear. They have a fascination with the rough aspect of the game, and they machine-gunned me with questions about it. I told them exactly how I felt. "I enjoy hitting. I'm talking about good, hard, clean hitting. I like to hit with a good, hard hip check and make guys on the other team keep their heads up."

Somebody said he felt sorry for me, signing with such a miserable club as the Islanders. I told him not to feel sorry; I kind of liked the idea of starting at the bottom. "Playing for a last-place team is a challenge for me. I enjoy such challenges. When I joined Ottawa, the club was in last place, but they soon became contenders. That's what I see the Islanders becoming soon."

# 8

# AN ISLANDER, AT LAST!

I was still pretty naive about the business of hockey business. Like the average sports fan, I believed what I read in the newspapers about salaries and signings. If a story said Joe Blow signed for $200,000 over a two-year period, I took it for granted that that *was* the deal. If a story said that two teams in two different leagues were bidding for the services of an athlete, I assumed that they *were,* in fact, competing for the player.

I was soon to learn that such was not always the case. What appeared in the papers was often the opposite of what was really taking place behind the closed doors of agents and hockey managers. It was a fascinating subject, and I learned fast. My first lesson came as I approached the homestretch of my final season of junior hockey.

Schatia had been holding a number of behind-the-scenes meetings with the Islanders while I was still playing for the 67s. A week or so before the draft Schatia and the Islanders had discussed terms (although I was soon to learn that I could very easily have landed in Montreal with the Canadiens). No mention of any deal was made right up to and after the moment that Bill Torrey signalled that I was his choice.

Soon after the Montreal meetings, Schatia and Sazant completed the deal and everyone—the lawyers, my brother, my parents—flew down to Long Island for another press conference, this one for the benefit of the New York media. Schatia revealed that we were working on a three-year contract with, as he put it, the complication that "there are still more contracts to sign. It has to be structured in such a way so that it will blend in smoothly the next time he signs. It's complicated when you're trying to provide for someone when he becomes 45 years old." I puffed on my meerschaum and listened.

Our "meeting" with the media took place at the Dover Inn, a restaurant in Westbury, Long Island, and again the questions came thick and fast.

"How much is he getting?" somebody shouted, and Schatia shot back just as quickly, "I'm an attorney. And anything between myself and my client is privileged."

Somebody asked me how to pronounce my name. "Pronounce it Dennis or Denee," I said, "anyway you want to, just so long as you spell it with one n."

My mother and father were at my side and they seemed to enjoy the confrontation as much as I did. "Denis is leaving home for the first time," my mother told a reporter, sounding very much like a mother. She then told the guy she wondered whether I'd be able to take care of myself. Imagine that for motherly concern!

This meeting with the media turned out just as well as the first one had. The next day I picked up the New York *Daily News* and read the handline: A POISED POTVIN MEETS N.Y. PRESS—IT'S A DRAW. So I was two-for-two. Not bad. But I knew all these headlines would be forgotten when training camp began in September and the big-league men were separated from the boys.

My own first move in that direction was a bit of extravagance: I bought myself a $14,900 Mercedes-Benz 450 SL just before leaving for training camp in Peterborough, Ontario. I don't usually get hung up with material things, but this car was something else. I couldn't wait to get it on the road. The trip to camp would be my first long ride with my car, and I decided to leave Ottawa early in the morning when there was nobody on the road and I could enjoy a leisurely spin.

The time came to make the big move. I said good-bye to the folks; it was a bit wrenching, but I was a big boy now and had to make the break. I took my gear, my golf clubs, just about everything I owned, tossed it in the back of the car, turned on the ignition, and I was on the road. Peterborough, here I come—maybe a little *too* fast.

For a short time my enthusiasm for this new hunk of sports car got the best of me, and I found myself testing the motor just to see how much power it really had. The next thing I knew, I looked down at the speedometer and saw the needle passing 130 m.p.h. I had no idea I was going that fast because the car moved along so easily.

I don't remember ever feeling more exuberant, more excited, and more proud of myself than I did as I tooled along to Peterborough. Oh, sure, there would be a lot of pressure to make good and to live up to the headlines, but somehow none of this seemed to weigh heavily on me. One thing that helped was the fact that the Islanders were training at Peterborough, where I had played for nearly six years and I felt right at home. I also knew that even if there was hostility from the other players, there *would* be the warmth of brother Jean. If all else failed, I knew I could go directly to Jean, as I always did when things got rough, and say, Okay, brother, what do we do now? More than anything, that removed any worries I might normally have had under the circumstances.

Before I knew it, I was pulling the Mercedes into the parking lot of Peterborough's Holiday Inn, checking into my room, and meeting Jean. It was 1969 all over again; the only difference was our Fu Manchus.

As I had hoped, Jean made me feel right at home. And so did a few other guys, like André St. Laurent, whom I had known after playing against him in junior hockey. I can't deny that it was a big lift for me to know there was a large contingent of French-Canadians in camp. There were Richard Grenier, Germain Gagnon, Gerry Desjardins, St. Laurent, and my brother.

There was no mistaking that I still felt my French-Canadian identity. Finding myself a minority among the English-Canadian majority inevitably brought out whatever prejudicial feelings I carried with me from childhood. (I don't think I ever experienced any hostility on that count at the Islanders' camp.) Just having a large bloc of French-Canadians around to lean on gave me the boost I needed.

Another boost was my own condition. I had worked out for several weeks before camp opened, and I felt good physically and mentally. What mattered now was how the other players felt about me. Their acceptance of the Number One Rookie—or their lack of acceptance— could make or break me. The guy who turned it all around was captain Eddie Westfall.

When I was eight years old Eddie Westfall was already in the NHL, skating for the Boston Bruins. Eddie had done it all; he played for the bad Boston teams in the early sixties and then, when Bobby Orr turned things around, he skated for the Bruins' Stanley Cup winners in 1970 and 1972. The Islanders drafted him in June 1972 and he immediately gave the team, no matter how many games it lost, a large touch of class.

Westfall's reaction to me would be pivotal; he was to arrive the day after I got to camp. We were in the lobby of the Holiday Inn when Eddie strode in, the usual big grin on his face. He spotted me immediately. Our eyes met and I awaited his reaction. It was quick and warm. "Welcome to the Islanders!" he shouted, pumped my hand, and before I knew it invited me out for a round of golf. How could I refuse?

Eddie and I became good friends right from the start. It was a tremendous feeling, having an old pro like Westfall treat a raw rookie like his brother. He impressed me more than anyone else on the team.

With the exception of goalie Gerry Desjardins (you *always* excuse a goaltender for idiosyncrasies simply because he *is* doing the most dangerous job in sports), the guys were pleasant to me up and down the line. I sensed right away that Desjardins' reaction to me was cold and distinctly different from that of the other fellows. But any flak he may have thought of giving me was stopped by the very presence of brother Jean. I stuck close to Jean at first, trying hard to be careful and to go unnoticed until I could meld securely with the gang.

That's why I was hypersensitive about a number of the personalities I had heard about but never met. Players like Garry Howatt. He had the reputation of a toy tiger, a little guy with lots of strength who liked nothing better than to fight. What would happen if Howatt played the wise guy and started challenging me as soon as we met? I found out soon enough. I walked to the dressing room, opened the door, and there, sitting across the room and putting on his gear, was Howatt himself. He just stuck out his hand and said, "Hi, Denis. I'm Garry Howatt. How're ya doing? Take a seat anywhere." Toy tiger. He was more like David Niven.

One by one the guys trooped in, and I found that they all were pretty decent, mostly young players. I could sense that a lot of them were curious about me, and I suppose they were anxious to test me to see if all that ink I had received was deserved. After Desjardins, the most distant of my teammates at first was Gerry Hart, a short, muscular defenseman with eyes that pierce like searchlights. I later discovered that Hart was one of the most articulate and thoughtful members of the team, but it took some time to make that discovery. My first impression was that Gerry didn't want to meet anybody new on the club, least of all big-shot Denis Potvin. I suspect that he was worried about me in particular because there always was the chance that I'd take his job away from him. After all, was there any way—short of complete collapse—that I wasn't going to make the club? Even a solid hockey player such as Hart must have had a lot of doubts. Slowly, but perceptibly, he began to come around and to be more friendly. I didn't want to rush him. I could sense it when Gerry was about to start up conversations and, pretty soon, we'd find ourselves sitting across a restaurant table having long talks because we learned that we had a lot of mutual interests.

Of all the stories about me that had given me trouble, the worst was an article, "Hit Man," in *The Canadian*. The head below the title proclaimed: BIG LEAGUES WATCH OUT—HERE COMES DENIS POTVIN. The article spelled out in detail what a tough guy I was supposed to be and how I had mauled Fran McKey in that game with St. Catherines. I heard, too, that our manager Bill Torrey had told a few of the other players that I was going to be the toughest guy in the NHL, based on my reputation in the OHA junior league. All these stories convinced me that a lot of guys would be trying me out for size at training camp just to see how tough I really was. So I had my guard up from the first scrimmage, but the reaction was much the same as it had been the first time I played against St. Catherines after the McKey incident—I simply wasn't harrassed. Not a bit.

The irony of it all was that Garry Howatt seemed determined to establish himself as the Islanders' "policeman," the player who would defend weaker players and take on the likes of Dave Schultz and other penalty leaders around the league. Garry thought that I would be giving him competition for the role of ice cop but I didn't want any part of it. "I don't mind fighting," I said, "in fact I used to enjoy it in the juniors, where I took out a lot of my frustrations. But I'd rather play the game." He understood.

*Machismo,* however unconscious, is a big thing among professional hockey players, and I expected one of the other rookies to put me to the test. The closest I came to an uprising, however, occurred during a scramble in front of the net. About five players were milling around and one of them—I don't know who—was holding my stick. It infuriated me. I dropped my stick, dropped my gloves, and was ready to go, but play continued and the anger was over in a second. Yet the incident was meaningful to me because I knew that the guys on the bench had seen what had happened and figured, Denis will fight if he has to.

As part of my goal to gain the respect of the guys on the team, I took care not to separate myself from the club. I made a point to be with the rest of the gang whenever possible, and I watched the little encounters between the players with a mixture of amusement and surprise.

One of the more amusing incidents occurred in the selection of numbers for jerseys. When there was a dispute, the final arbiter was trainer Nick Garen. Brian Spencer, an intense, hyperactive sort, wanted number 15—as did Billy Harris, the Islanders' top draft pick. Manager Bill Torrey wanted the argument settled as amicably as possible and asked Garen to use his best diplomacy.

Garen did a masterful job. As Spencer passed the dressing room, the trainer pulled jersey number nine out of a box. "Do you know what team I was a trainer with for 23 years?" he asked.

"Sure," said Spencer, "the Chicago Black Hawks."

"That's right," said Garen. "And do you know who wore number nine there? Bobby Hull. And do you know who wore number nine in Detroit? Gordie Howe. And do you know who wore it in Montreal? Of course, Rocket Richard."

Hearing a promotion like that, Spencer grabbed the number nine jersey from Garen and was much happier with it than number 15.

I was hoping to wear number seven, but that number already belonged to Germain Gagnon, a "veteran" of one year with the Islanders, so I settled for number five without a fuss.

More important for me, at this point, was proving myself. I wanted to earn in play every cent they were paying me. And I think I got carried away the first week of training camp. I was so eager to make good that I decided to ignore a throbbing charleyhorse that probably should have put me on the sidelines. One day I came to camp limping pretty badly. A lot of people, including Torrey, must have thought I'd take the day off. Instead, I suited up and skated through the whole session. It was a good move on my part. The next day, Red Burnett quoted Torrey in *The Toronto Star:* "We're just delighted with his attitude and willingness to work."

The guy I was most concerned about was Al Arbour, the coach. I had met Al briefly during the summer and was impressed by his warm smile. (For some reason I notice a smile more than I do other features.) Al seemed to be a good—but hard—person who made me feel comfortable the way Leo Boivin did in my last year of junior hockey.

"I'm worried about you," Arbour told me the first time we sat down together at camp. "You're overweight by at least ten pounds. How come?"

"I can't explain it," I told him. "I worked out all summer and I feel good, although maybe a little slower than I should be."

"Look," he said, "I'm goin' to be harder on you than I am on some of the other guys."

That was okay with me. I wasn't afraid of *not* making the team;

Torrey had already assured me on that score. "Just play your game," said Torrey. "Take your time coming along if you want, but be ready for the season."

Torrey had a very comforting effect on me, and I felt relaxed as we opened the exhibition season. If I made a mistake, well, it was done with and I'd make up for it next time. I knew that people would resent me. It would be either resentment, envy, or hate. My first contact with those sentiments came after our first exhibition game with the New York Rangers.

# 9

# DENIS POTVIN vs. BRAD PARK, BRYAN WATSON, AND DAVE SCHULTZ

I first met Brad Park at a cocktail party that followed a golf tournament involving a lot of hockey players. Park and I had only the most casual of meetings. My reaction to him was not particularly warm. By September of 1973, he was the reigning defenseman of the New York Rangers and I was the top rookie defenseman on the Islanders.

I'm not sure how Park felt about me before our first game at Nassau Coliseum, but I knew that he lived on Long Island and I knew that he read *Newsday* and I figured he must have read what Jean had said about me prior to that first exhibition game.

"After Denis drops his man," Jean said, "I'm going to skate up to the poor guy and say, 'You mean you let a 19-year-old kid kick the spit out of you. Tsk, tsk.' That may start another fight, but who cares. I've got Denis on my side."

That made good "copy" for the newspapers, but it also served to antagonize the opposition. Coaches just love to read such stories as that; they paste them up on the dressing room bulletin board to get their own team good and mad. As a result, I expected the Rangers would give me more trouble than usual.

They were impressive when they skated out in their blue jerseys with R-A-N-G-E-R-S in red lettering across the front. I studied the stars— Rod Gilbert, Jean Ratelle, and Brad Park—and found myself feeling a bit apprehensive, as any other rookie would in the same situation. I found I was muttering to myself. Uh-oh, there's Gilbert! I was tight and far too much in awe of these guys.

Once the puck was dropped, I seemed to be skating in mud. (One writer said, "Denis seemed confused at first.") But as I loosened up my game improved. The Rangers led 3–0 and 4–1, then I got hot: two shots and two goals! The crowd went wild and I was tempted to take more chances, but I deliberately held back. Minnesota coach Jackie Gordon was there and said later, "I'm glad to see a kid with all his talent isn't trying to be another Bobby Orr." Nor a Brad Park.

Park didn't give me any grief, but he got some from my teammate Bobby Nystrom who belted Brad around in the third period. Park went to the ice with blood in his left eye. Nystrom's decision over Park was symbolic: The Islanders proved that they could take the best of the Rangers both on the scoreboard and in the fight department. We fought from behind and came off with a 6–6 tie—and made quite an impression on the fans and the media. Unfortunately, we didn't seem to make an impression on Park. And apparently some of the more childish Rangers had made a pact before the game not to answer obvious press questions about their first impressions of Denis Potvin.

Hugh Delano of *The New York Post* approached Park in the Rangers' room after the game, prepared to ask the inevitable question. "I know what you're goin' to ask me," Park snapped. He opened a copy of the program. "See 'What Do You Think of Denis Potvin?' right here in this magazine. I wrote it *before* the game."

What *did* Park think of me? He told Delano that he wanted to wait and see me play again before making any judgment. "I'll reserve my decision for now," he said.

A few minutes later Delano walked into our dressing room and relayed Park's comments. Then he asked me what I thought of Park. My first opportunity to get involved in a juicy NHL controversy! "Obviously," I said, "Park's a good defenseman. But tonight he was not as aggressive as I expected him to be. Maybe that's because he thought he was playing against the Islanders and we'd be a pushover. I have mixed feelings about Park, but I'll hold back whatever other feelings I have until a later date."

Delano seemed surprised that I bothered to take the time to talk at length with him. He said that players on other teams—the Rangers included—couldn't wait to undress, shower, "dress and stampede through the dressing room door for post-game beer and broads."

I let him know that I didn't want to be a big, dumb hockey player. I didn't want to fit the mold of the leather-headed jock who thinks sports and money are the end-all of life on earth. "Your questions don't bother me," I said. "I enjoy talking. I have my job, you have yours. I can help you, you can help me. A professional athlete has an obligation to answer questions. Fans like to know what the players have to say."

I could tell that Delano was down on the Rangers and their attitude. He had seen some of them rip tape recorders from newsmen's hands, ruin interviews by deliberately shouting obscenities, bully sportswriters who tell it like it is, and, worst of all, hide from interviews in showers and training rooms. "Such things," Delano said, "have been known to happen at a popular local rink in Manhattan."

Fine, let the Rangers make boors of themselves and antagonize the writers. I wasn't going to take that route—and my attitude came through. On October 6, 1973, the first really dazzling column about me appeared in a New York daily. It was Delano's "Working Press" column in *The New York Post,* it was titled "Modest Superstar," and it downgraded the Rangers and their decision not to answer questions about me.

"Their [the Rangers'] opinions were unnecessary," wrote Delano. "It was obvious that the Islanders have their own version of the Nets' exciting Dr. J."

The words were sweet music to me. I was feeling better game by game, training myself not to be awed by the big names around me and I was developing confidence. I could sense two personalities working inside me: Denis Potvin the person and Denis Potvin the hockey player. Before a game I could feel my fingers and legs twitching for contact and victory. I could sense a certain self-assurance. I was hungry on the ice (something I couldn't accuse the Rangers of) and off the ice I had another kind of confidence. Instead of hitting or controlling the play, I talked. And whomever I talked with seemed to be an equal; nobody made me feel inferior.

It was that way after the regular season started. We opened at The Omni in Atlanta and played the Flames to a 1–1 tie. At last I really felt I was in the big time. When the final buzzer sounded I was as tired as I had ever been in my life. Arbour had me on the ice for 40 minutes, and I really felt it. The experience was a whole new hockey game. By comparison, playing junior hockey had been a breeze; when I moved an inch I could make a few yards, and shoving one guy with my arm would make the entire opposition shy away. Now, when I hit someone on the Atlanta team, I felt something go out of my body. It hurt!

That was good. I would have been disappointed if the NHL had been too easy on me at the start. I needed the challenge and I felt a new drive inside me, pushing me, pushing me. I wanted to keep going up, and to do that I felt I had to be mean. And a few members of the loyal opposition helped to bring out this meanness in me.

Brad Park, partly because he was a Ranger, and partly because he had been an All-Star and I aspired to that position, was one opponent who got me good and mad. Bryan "Bugsy" Watson of the Detroit Red Wings was another.

Bugsy's nickname was well earned. As defensemen go, Watson is relatively small, but he's absolutely fearless and loves to fight. He "bugs" because he's always talking or hitting—or both. When he first tested me, Watson was still playing for Pittsburgh. We were in the Penguins' home rink when our collision took place. I was carrying the puck along the right side and tried to swoop around him for a shot on goal. Watson kept backtracking, but I found an opening, took my shot, and then swerved at the corner to get back to my defensive position.

Once I had taken the shot, I relaxed my muscles momentarily, feeling that all was clear. It wasn't. The next moment the world turned black. I barely recall seeing the outline of Watson's thickly ribbed leather gauntlet and his stick simultaneously crease me in the head.

Luckily, I was dazed only for a second and Watson was still in the vicinity when I recovered my senses. Well, I said to myself, this is it! I dropped my gloves and began swinging—and connecting. Watson soon put his head down and tried to bore it through my stomach. That was a signal to the linesmen to move in and separate us, which they did. I was pleased with myself on two counts: I survived my first attack from behind and I had given Bugsy a good going-over. My first NHL fight was a success.

Sooner or later I knew that I would have to face "the Dave Schultz test." Schultz had earned the reputation as one of the most eager fighters in the NHL; they called him "The Hammer" in Philadelphia because of his quick fists. What annoyed me when we played Philadelphia was that I found myself almost obsessed with Schultz. I was constantly aware of his position on the ice, and I knew that I shouldn't be so concerned with him.

Our run-in took place at Nassau Coliseum the first time we played the Flyers. Schultz had picked up good speed, moving down left wing (my right side), and tried to squeeze between me and the sideboards. There was no way I was going to let Schultz get past me or avoid hitting him, and I made that perfectly synchronized move, when body meets body, when a defenseman is happier sending an opponent to the ice than scoring a goal. Schultz crumpled like cardboard on impact, simultaneously freezing the puck against the boards for a face-off.

I skated back to my position to await the next face-off. Meanwhile, Schultz clambered to his skates, but instead of taking his spot on the line he came over to me, holding his stick high, around my eyes. Now when something like this happens, and the potential perpetrator is a guy with Schultz's reputation, you have to worry. He might start swinging where it could hurt.

Fortunately, I stayed cool. I stared back at him and said, "Go fuck yourself. If you want me, come get me now."

This was my first High Noon confrontation. The others had been kid stuff. Bugsy Watson, for all his toughness, was not really that menacing; Schultz had a reputation, and he was not the kind of character to relish embarrassment before a big crowd.

The Hammer didn't accept my invitation. He just skated away and never bothered me again that night. But what he might do on his home rink perplexed me. Lots of times players who are lambs on the road turn into lions before the home crowd. So, when we next visited The Spectrum in Philadelphia, I was well aware that Schultz might just give me trouble.

I was right. This time the battle erupted in the corner near our net as I rubbed him into the boards. He lifted his stick, pushed it against my head, and put his glove in my face. Since the puck was at my feet, I ignored him until I had moved the rubber out of our zone. By then he had moved a few feet away from me, so I shouted some obscenity at him. Instead of moving in the other direction, as he had been doing, Schultz wheeled in his tracks and snapped a challenge: "Do you want to go?"

"Okay, let's go!"

Down went the gloves and up came the fists. We both threw them fast at first, but then Schultz's boxing-hockey expertise came to the fore. As I threw a right cross, he came back and grabbed my right arm, tying me up. Then he hit me a couple of hard ones. I wised up just in time and began whacking him with my left. I knew I had hurt him just by the feel on my fist. Then I pinned him against the boards and we wrestled each other to the ice. This was the signal for the linesmen to move in and pull us apart, and I was delighted that they did.

I skated off the ice with mixed emotions. I was upset with myself because I hadn't fought well and he had caught me with a few solid blows. I felt I had lost the fight, and that embarrassed me. On the other hand, I felt pretty good because, after all the thinking about Schultz, I finally ended it by slugging it out with him. I began to feel better and better, the more I thought about it. Sonofabitch, I said to myself, he's only human.

The other Islanders had just come into the dressing room at the end of the period. I could sense that they were curious about my reaction to the fight.

"Well, guys," I shouted across the room, "I'll tell you something about Dave Schultz: My old lady can punch a lot harder than he can."

# 10

## A TROPHY FOR BREAKFAST

I remember, when I was a kid, reading in my history book about December 7, 1941, Pearl Harbor Day, and how Franklin Delano Roosevelt, the President of the United States, described it as "a day of infamy." The word "infamy" always intrigued me. The phrase "day of infamy" was even more awesome in its suggestion of disaster. I used to wonder whether Denis Potvin would ever be involved in a situation like that.

After December 16, 1973, I had to wonder no more. Denis Potvin, who wanted only to be famous, suddenly became the infamous man of hockey.

Sunday morning, December 16, 1973, was not a typical Sunday. It was cold, dark, and wet, with a feel of snow in the air. From what others tell me, there was an aura of pre-dawn throughout the day. I can't testify about the weather conditions prior to 10 A.M. because, unfortunately, I was snug in bed, very fast asleep.

We had played a home game with the Chicago Black Hawks the night before, and I was really beat. But that is no excuse for what happened. When I got home Saturday night, I knew we had a game at The Spectrum in Philadelphia the following night, and I was well aware that the Islanders' bus was to leave from Nassau Coliseum at exactly 10 A.M. for the ride to Philly. With that in mind, I set my alarm clock for 9 A.M., which would give me enough time to have a quick breakfast, get dressed, and drive to the rink.

To this day I'm not quite sure what happened to the alarm. Either I didn't set it right or it did go off and I simply shut it off and went back to sleep. All I know is that I don't recall hearing the alarm.

The first sound I heard was at 9:50 A.M. It was the telephone, and it kept ringing and ringing. My head was so out of it that I assumed the hour was somewhere between seven and eight. If the phone hadn't kept ringing, I probably would have stayed in bed, I was that groggy. But it didn't stop.

Finally, grudgingly, I threw off the blanket and sheets, slid out of bed, and picked up the receiver. If the caller had been a reporter, I'd have told him to go to hell; if it had been a wrong number, I'd have slammed down the receiver; if it had been coach Arbour, I'd have counted to ten and tried to talk like a reasonable person.

"Hello!" I snapped.

"Denis, where the fuck are you? The bus is leaving in ten minutes—move your ass!"

It was Bobby Nystrom. He told me Arbour was pacing the aisle of the bus, glancing at his watch every second or two, and was going to give the driver the signal pretty soon.

"Tell him I'll be outa here in a minute," I shouted, and hung up.

I ran around like a wild man, throwing on my clothes. I dashed out of the house, jumped in the car, and tried to cover the six miles in five minutes. Snow had begun to fall. The highway was wet and I was slipping like a drunken stunt driver. I looked at the fuel gauge and it showed just a spit over empty.

But there was enough gas to take me to the rink. At the last crossing before the Coliseum I was stopped by a red light. I waited. When it changed I zoomed into the parking lot.

My radio blared: "W-I-N-S news time, ten-oh-six."

Geez, I thought to myself, I might make it after all.

I looked around the parking lot but saw no sign of a bus. I looked for someone, anyone. A tall black guy from the Nets basketball team walked across the lot. Before I could say a word, he looked at me and chirped, "Hey, man, the bus is gone!"

"You're kidding," I said.

"No, man, the bus *is* gone."

I panicked. My first reaction was to go to the locker room. I dashed across the wet, snowy parking lot and down the gray concrete steps to the Coliseum basement. The sign on the door said "New York Islanders." The door was locked.

By now all kinds of crazy things were running through my head, one clouding over the other. What have I done? . . . What will the guys think? . . . How will the coach react? . . . Are the newspaper guys goin' to ruin me for this? . . . Did my alarm ever go off?

I returned slowly to the parking lot, trying to get hold of myself. All right, Denis, keep your head. You have to figure out what to do now.

When I reached my Mercedes the snow was coming down hard and it looked like a blizzard was in the works. Should I drive to Philly? I asked myself.

I rejected the idea. We were in the midst of a fuel crisis. Gas was impossible to obtain on a Sunday morning. Besides, my tank hardly had enough gas in it to get me back to my apartment. I'll go back home, I decided, and wait for *somebody* to call.

I had no idea who that somebody might be. For some inexplicable reason I thought maybe Bill Torrey's secretary, Estelle Ellery, or someone else connected with the team would ring me and help out. I didn't want to be away from my phone.

I got back to the apartment, took off my wet clothes, and sat looking at the telephone, hoping my stares would stimulate it to ring. Not a sound.

The minutes became hours. I tried to phone Estelle at the Islanders' office, but it was closed. I tried to find her home number in the telephone directory, but I couldn't. Now I was in a frenzy, trying to call anyone, but nobody was home. I was panicking again.

If I had thought clearly, I would have phoned Ray Volpe, who then was a vice president in the NHL New York office and a good friend. I knew his number and I'm sure, if I had phoned Ray, he would have worked something out for me. He might have told me what I didn't know—that I could catch a train from Penn Station to Philly, hire a car, or anything but sit in the house.

Sure, I could have tried to get to Manhattan on my own. But I was still very naive about the city. I had never been alone in Manhattan, I didn't know my way around, and I was afraid I'd get lost. And now the snow was coming down so hard it really looked like a blizzard; no planes would fly in this weather.

So I sat in my empty living room and waited. And waited. At six o'clock the phone finally rang. I was so excited I practically grabbed the receiver on the first "ping." It was Jean. He was calling from The Spectrum.

"What in hell are you doin' at home?"

How could I answer that? I told him I didn't know what to do.

"I'll tell you what to do—get on a train and get down here, man; you'll be able to suit up for the second period."

Before I could say another word, Jean handed the phone to the coach.

"What the hell did you do?"

I told him the whole story.

"Okay," said Al. "Just stay there. Don't move out of your house tonight. But be at practice, ready to go on the ice, at ten tomorrow morning." And he hung up.

Arbour's voice was cutting. As soon as he had hung up I began reading into his command. I was really afraid I had managed to screw up my career at age 20. I had had ten hours to get to Philadelphia from New York, a two-hour trip by car, and I wound up watching the game on television. Beautiful.

At 7 P.M. the game started and within ten minutes Rick MacLeish had shot the puck past Gerry Desjardins. I walked over to the TV and flicked the picture off. I couldn't stand watching them anymore. Then I turned it back on to discover that Dave Fortier, a tough young defenseman, was skating in my place. Before the first period was over, Philly was leading, 2–0. I shut it off again, but I couldn't stand *not* watching it, so I turned it on for the second period and watched Don Saleski and Bill Clement pump two more past Desjardins.

If that wasn't bad enough, I had to watch Hawley Chester, the Islanders' publicity man, do the "color" commentary between the second and third periods. Instead of keeping quiet about my absence, Hawley said, "Denis missed the bus and didn't even bother showing up for the game."

I nearly flew out of my chair and punched him in the mouth on the TV screen. He was adding fuel to the fire I had started, and I was simultaneously furious and in a state of shock.

At last the game was over. We lost, 4–0, keeping intact our record of never having won on the road. What the score might have been if I had made the bus was irrelevant. I missed it and I would have to pay the consequences in the morning.

Actually, I began paying for my mistake that night. A few minutes after the game had ended, the first of several calls came from the newspapermen. I described what had happened and I waited to see what the headlines would say the next day. I was up early on Monday morning—I *had* to be—and picked up *Newsday:* POTVIN, GAME WERE LOST. The *Daily News* put it another way: A SAD STORY BY AWOL POTVIN.

Somebody had asked Freddie Shero, coach of the Flyers, about my absence. "Maybe all that money and publicity went to his head," said Shero. By nine on Monday morning I figured I was the most humiliated athlete in the world.

I arrived at the Coliseum dressing room at 9:15. Nobody was there. I walked to my cubicle and began putting on my gear. There was a strange quiet about the place—just me, the uniforms, and the pervasive smell of liniment. I was early, but nobody was around to tell me what to do, so I just waited. At 9:50, exactly 24 hours after I had gotten the infamous wake-up call, Al walked into the room. I waited for some kind of acknowledgment, even a grunted "hello," but he strolled past me without a word and disappeared. The dressing room was empty again and I wondered what the hell was going on. All of a sudden the trainer popped his head in and shouted: "Denis, get on the ice in five minutes!"

My skates were laced in a minute. I walked across the black rubber mat, turned right at the entranceway, and moved past the seats to the ice. I wondered, What's he going to pull on me next? I took a few easy skates around the rink and then Al jumped on the ice. He was wearing an orange jacket and blue sweat pants. "All right," he said, "line up at the end boards!" I knew now what was going to happen.

"Start skating. Up and down, back and forth." For a solid hour he put me through every conceivable drill. There was still no one else in the rink and I figured maybe I'd be through with this before the other guys arrived. I was worried about their reactions.

Al kept on. It seemed interminable. A few figures appeared at the corner near the dressing room; the players were arriving. Some of them walked up to the ice entrance. I could see them shake their heads. They went into the dressing room, suited up, and soon the team was ready for a full-dress drill.

I sensed mixed feelings among the players, but nothing was said during the scrimmage; it was as if the entire incident was closed. But it wasn't. The minute we finished the workout I got a message to report to Bill Torrey's office. He wanted to know precisely what had happened and I told him exactly what I told Al and some of the reporters. I had screwed up.

After listening, Torrey very calmly said, "Well, Denis, I'm going to have to fine you. But there's something much more important about this whole thing as far as you're concerned. You'll have to go to the players and apologize for not being in Philly and for letting them down."

This wasn't going to be easy. The critiques, by this time, were flowing thick and fast. One NHL star, who didn't want his name used, accused me of missing the game because I was "probably afraid of playing against the Flyers in The Spectrum." I agreed with Bill that I'd apologize to the guys the next day in the dressing room.

I wanted to get the whole thing over with as quickly as possible because the incident had just knocked me out mentally. So, 48 hours after it happened, I stood in front of my pals and said it plain and simple: "I goofed. I'm sorry about it, and I can assure you it'll never happen again. When the alarm goes off now, I'll get my butt out of the bed, damn quick! Listen, guys, I apologize for doing such a stupid thing."

Like an actor awaiting the reviews of his first night on Broadway, I watched for the reaction. Eddie Westfall smiled. "Next time, Baby Bear won't hibernate in his house." The guys laughed. Once I saw the smiles on veterans like Germain Gagnon and Craig Cameron, I felt the worst was over. After that everybody on the team was really good about it—at least to me—and nobody made a big thing about it; there were no more smart comments after the apology.

Torrey was pleased that I had taken his advice, but he was concerned that I was still worrying about the episode. After I had spoken to the players, he took me aside again. "Denis," he said, "it's over and done with. You've paid for it physically and monetarily, so we're not going to talk about it any more."

He was good for his word. Neither Bill nor Al nor the players talked about it anymore, and I made a point of not reading a newspaper for three weeks. If it had turned out any other way, if the players had gotten good and angry and rebelled against me, the whole hockey world could have crashed down on my head. Instead, the pervasive feeling was "no problem," and after three or four days the incident seemed like an event of the dim past.

I still thought a lot about it. I thought to myself, These people have really been nice to me, so I've got to come up big for them. I realized I couldn't second-guess myself, that I had to redouble my efforts to be the best. From that point on, I accentuated the positive—and it became the turning point in my career. A few weeks later I was on the ice at Chicago Stadium, a starting defenseman in the NHL All-Star Game. Not bad for a 20-year-old who had missed the bus!

Among the mistakes I've made, missing the team bus was about my worst. Believe it or not, I came awfully close to doing it again on New Year's Day 1974.

We suffered through a really dull workout early that morning at the practice rink in Kings Park and were told to report at the Holiday Inn in

Westbury before 2 P.M. That was the time our bus was scheduled to leave for LaGuardia Airport and our 15th road trip of the season, this time to Chicago.

I was still feeling woozy from New Year's Eve and probably should have left home earlier than 1:45 P.M. But traffic was light, the drive took only ten minutes, and I pulled into the motel parking lot with two minutes to spare. When I took my seat in the bus it was 30 seconds before 2 P.M.

I'm sure nothing more would have come of it, were it not for one reporter on the bus, Tim Moriarty of *Newsday,* who decided it was news. He sat next to me and asked if I had been worried about missing the bus.

"Not really," I told him. "I don't live very far from here."

"What time did you leave your apartment?" he persisted.

I was getting the third degree, but enough time had passed since the debacle in December that I could stay cool throughout the questioning.

"You cut it pretty close this time," he said.

I smiled, "I wasn't worried."

That ended the conversation, but Moriarty wasn't through. He went to the coach and asked about the December incident, the $500 fine Al had slapped me with, and my reaction.

Arbour didn't mince words. "Missing the bus left a mark on Denis," he said. "He won't admit it, but he was a little uptight for the next few games. He was concerned about the stories and what the fans would think. He didn't want people to think he was irresponsible.

"To me, that was a good sign. He could have taken the other route, another outlook, and said the hell with the fine and the fans. But that wouldn't be Denis Potvin. He does care—about the way he plays hockey and about what people think. He hasn't missed a team bus since."

It was gratifying to have the coach in my corner. I know that a lot of other NHL coaches have been resentful of high-priced rookies. If I had been stuck with a guy with that kind of attitude, I would have been in real trouble.

Another guy who backed me up when I needed it was brother Jean. He had kept quietly in the background through my first couple of months in the league, but he finally popped off in the middle of the 1973–74 season when a couple of people became critical of my play.

"I know Denis has made some mistakes," Jean told Jerry Cassidy of the *Daily News,* "but show me someone who doesn't make mistakes. It isn't Denis' fault that some people built him up to be another Bobby Orr. I'm fed up with people magnifying his every mistake. For crying out loud, the kid's only 20!"

That was pretty heavy talk for a light-hearted guy like Jean, and it did me a world of good.

So did the nomination to the 1974 All-Star Game. That was really something—to arrive at the Chicago Stadium dressing room to find myself surrounded by the likes of Yvan Cournoyer, Red Berenson, Mickey Redmond, Ken Dryden, and Frank Mahovlich. Coach for the East Division team was Scotty Bowman, and just before game time he came over to me and said, "You're going to work with Brad Park." My legs were quivering with excitement.

I had mixed emotions about my partner. I wasn't crazy about Brad Park the person, but Brad Park the player was still top quality. The moment we got on the ice we seemed to meld well together, talking to each other whenever possible.

In the third period, with the score 5–2 for the West, I grabbed the puck about 45 feet from the net. Tony Esposito was in goal for the West, and I think he figured I was going to pass instead of shoot. I got off a pretty hard slapshot that screened him. Next thing I knew the red light was on. I'll never forget that thrill! It was so stupendous, so unreal, I could never put it into words.

The goal was a big boost. But still bigger was the comment coach Bowman made after the game: "Denis was my best defenseman tonight; he played a great game."

Then I got the most surprising "present" of all. Park, who had been so reticent to say anything about me at the start of the season, began talking as though he were my personal press agent. "Denis is my choice for rookie-of-the-year," Park said. "He's tough and he's not afraid to throw his weight around."

But the Islanders, as a team, wasn't doing as well in the homestretch of 1973–74 as Denis Potvin, and it was depressing. At times we went up against weaker teams when we clearly weren't giving our best efforts. Some guys decided to quit because of our position in the standings, but I couldn't condone that.

I had my personal ups and downs, but I developed self-confidence in the course of the season. I found I had to stand up and shout inside. I found I couldn't afford to let little things get me down. I knew that if I wanted to be the best, I'd have to think that way. And I kept on thinking it, and I took dead aim on winning the NHL's Calder Memorial Trophy as rookie-of-the-year.

The scariest episode in my rookie year, after the embarrassment and trauma induced by my missing the team bus, was a near death-blow caused by a flying puck.

Time and again I hear people criticize players for using helmets. Whenever it happens, I recall that game at the Vancouver Coliseum and the 100-mile-per-hour drive that Canucks defenseman Jocelyn Guevremont sent in my direction.

I was standing in front of our net when Guevremont, one of the NHL's hardest shooters, captured the puck on his stick. "Josh" wound up and I heard the crack of wood against rubber. But I lost sight of the black blur between the moment of impact and the moment the puck nearly sailed *into* my eye.

When I realized that the puck was coming at me, it was only five inches from my eye. I did the only thing I could do: I turned away from the missile, but not far enough; the puck smashed into my helmet just above my right ear. All I remember is hearing bells and bells and what sounded like the entire carillon of St. Patrick's Cathedral.

I blacked out for several minutes, then found myself in the infirmary where the doctor was administering smelling salts and telling me what a lucky guy I was for wearing a protective headpiece.

He reached across the rubbing table and handed the helmet to me.

"Do you see what I see?" he asked.

What I saw was a huge crack up and down the side of the helmet. The velocity of Guevremont's shot had been so great that the puck had actually cracked this toughest of all protective plastic.

The doctor winked at me. "Denis," he said, "if you weren't wearing this thing, you'd have been dead."

But I was very much alive—and kicking. My confidence returned, and this self-confidence paid off. I never really doubted that I could win the Calder. There were times when I said, Hey, slow down. But I never did slow down. I wanted to keep going, knowing I had to beat out Tom Lysiak and Borje Salming for the prize.

Lysiak, a big center from Medicine Hat, Alberta, would be my biggest threat. He was having an excellent season with the Atlanta Flames, but he wasn't getting the kind of ink that I was, mostly because I played in the New York area. Tony Andrea, a good friend who then worked for the NHL, told me near the end of the season: "Denis, you keep playing the way you are and there won't be any doubt that you'll be the top rookie. The greatest advantage you have is playing in the New York region. New York is the media capital. Anyone who plays here is automatically better known around the league."

The annual NHL awards are made every year during the June league meetings in Montreal. For hockey people it is like a convention. Everyone from coaches in the lowest minor leagues to presidents of NHL clubs meets there to discuss business, make trades, find jobs, and plan the season ahead. A highlight of the week-long activity is a banquet at which the prizes are distributed to members of the All-Star Team and to individual award winners.

The award winners are usually kept secret until a day or two before the ceremonies themselves, so until the Sunday before the meetings I had absolutely no idea how I had come out in the race with Lysiak and Salming. That Sunday morning I was sitting at the breakfast table at my parents' house when the phone rang.

My father answered it and spoke in English, something he didn't usually do in our house unless he was speaking to an English-speaking person who didn't know French. From the drift of Dad's conversation, I realized he was talking to Bill Torrey and Torrey was in Montreal. Dad gave me the receiver and I heard Bill ask, "Well, Denis, are you coming to Montreal to pick up your silverware?"

I was too overwhelmed to respond. I couldn't even handle a simple conversation. I gave the phone back to my father and began yelling and screaming like a baby. When I had finally calmed down, I told Bill I'd see him in Montreal on Tuesday. Then we returned to the table and finished breakfast with a bottle of Drambuie. By 11 A.M. we were all drunk.

A dream come true; that's brother Jean on the left, Dad, Islanders General Manager Bill Torrey and me. *(Photo by Joe Bereswill)*

A motherly kiss and hug after a big win.

Just out of the penalty box, 1954.

Ups and downs at the Ottawa rink.

One of my most memorable hat tricks. *(Bruce Bennett)*

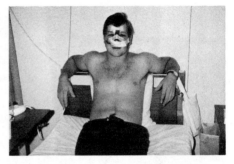

No, it's not Frankenstein, nor the Bionic Hockey Player. It's bloody Denis after a Junior mishap.

This is what it's all about—a fake, a backhander and a score against our rivals from across the county line. *(Bruce Bennett)*

This is why the Flyers occasionally get headaches. I learned when you go back to the bench, it's *FEET* first! *( Joe Bereswill)*

In case you're wondering, I'm shouting for joy as we beat Buffalo in the third game of the Stanley Cup Quarterfinals, spring, 1976. *(Bruce Bennett)*

My favorite team, 1976. *(Joe Bereswill)*

*Front Row (left to right):* Bill Smith, Ralph Stewart, Roy Boe (President), Coach Al Arbour, Captain
  Ed Westfall, Bill Torrey (General Manager), Bill Harris, Bert Marshall, Glenn Resch.
*Second Row:* Andre St. Laurent, Gerry Hart, Garry Howatt, Dave Fortier, Jude Drouin, J. P. Parise,
  Denis Potvin, Bryan Trottier.
*Third Row:* Ron Waske, Jean Potvin, Bill MacMillan, Bob Nystrom, Lorne Henning, Clark Gillies,
  Dave Lewis, Jim Pickard.

"Me! Two minutes?" *( Joe Bereswill and Bob*
*Pisano)*

Barreling through the Rangers' line.

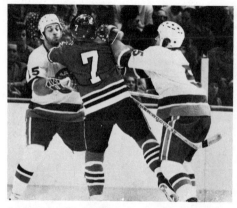 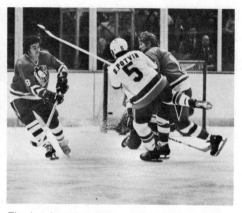

Sometimes it takes two men to stop an opponent as tough as Chicago's Pit Martin. Here I'm helping teammate Billy Harris prepare a "sandwich."

The hardest shot for a goaltender to stop is a screened shot. That's Vic Hadfield of Pittsburgh obliging me with the screen, but Gary Inness somehow managed to kick it out.

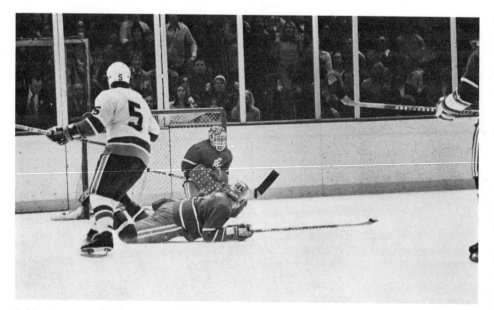

Taking my man out of the play and off the puck.

(Photos by Joe Bereswill)

Da or nyet? This time Soviet Wings' goalie Aleksandr Sidelnikov says "Nyet!"

Gary Dornhoefer of the Flyers is the toughest player to move from the goal crease. Here I'm starting from the top.

I wish this was all any goalie ever saw of me. (*Joe Bereswill*)

After scoring against the Philadelphia Flyers during the 1975–76 season, beaten goalie Wayne Stephenson turns around just in time to see me retrieve my 30th goal of the season. The fans gave me such a tremendous ovation when I returned to the bench that I cried. *(Joe Bereswill)*

My Boswell (Stan Fischler) interviewing my wife.

Jean and I embrace following a goal against our arch-rivals, the Rangers. ( *Joe Bereswill*)

# 11

# "I ALMOST GOT KILLED"

In my early days of junior hockey in Ottawa, I had an active social life. I love dancing and I used to go to the local teen-age dances as much as possible. When you're a junior hockey star, you're like the big man on campus at college, the football hero. There was no problem finding girls to go out with while I played for the 67s.

My social life didn't last long, though; when I was 16, I met a very beautiful 15-year-old girl at a club. From that point—with an occasional interruption—my social future was charted.

Debbie and I met, as I recall, in a bar in Ottawa. A friend and I were sitting at the bar watching a show when three girls came in. One of the girls knew my friend, and I remembered having seen them around. They sat with us and we began talking. (Although we had to be 21 to be in the bar, we both looked older, so we never had a problem in that respect.)

Debbie was tremendously attractive, and we soon found we had mutual interests. A few days later, I telephoned her and, to my dismay, she didn't even remember my name. But after talking awhile she recognized me, and I asked her if I could take her to the prom. She said yes.

Debbie didn't know at first that I was a hockey player. One evening I asked her to go to a hockey game. I took it for granted that she knew I was playing. At the rink she sat with one of my friends the whole damn time, waiting for me to come to the seat. And I heard later that she had nearly walked out of the building, she was so upset that I hadn't shown up.

Finally my friend said, "Debbie, don't you realize that Denis is out there playing?" That's the first she'd heard that I was a hockey player with the Ottawa 67s. After the game we all gathered in the arena lobby. She was really surprised, and sort of happy—but she also seemed embarrassed because she had been so disappointed when I hadn't shown up before the game.

We began going out once or twice a week. For one period of three or four months, we were also going out with different people. Once during those five years before we married Debbie went to Europe for a year, and several times we sort of split up and went our own ways for two or three months.

Her going overseas had a tremendous effect on our relationship because we were both at a point where we were looking to be by ourselves. When Debbie left we were good friends and we started writing to each other about three times a week. I wrote more letters than I had ever written in my life. Then we sent tape recordings to each other instead of letters. The longer she was away, the more I wanted her.

When she was in Europe I was in a situation much like the one she's in now. Now she says, "Denis, how come you don't miss me when you're on the road?"

I tell her, "I don't miss you as much because I'm kept very busy doing things like practicing and playing with the guys." But as a junior, with Debbie in Europe, I was the one at home and she was the one away and keeping busy.

It was April when Debbie came home, after some pleading from me, and our relationship became more and more solid. If we had been five or six years older we would probably have gotten married then. But there was still a period when we felt we wanted to get to know each other better. When I left for New York and my first NHL season, it was increasingly difficult for me to stay away from Debbie. I spent many of my nights just sitting around my apartment because there was nothing I could have enjoyed in New York without Debbie.

By the middle of my NHL rookie season, Debbie and I were so deeply in love that marriage had become my all-consuming thought. I decided to have a talk with my closest friend in New York, Ray Volpe, who worked at the NHL office.

Volpe, in his mid-thirties, is one of those rare individuals who sees things clearly and sees them whole. He was extremely cautious when I told him of my intention to get married. "Denis," he said, "there's one thing you have to be very sure of before you go the route. You have to be certain that you are the same person with Debbie as you are without her around."

That really started me thinking. Volpe explained that there are celebrities who develop dual personalities: One they wear when they're with their wife or their girlfriend and the other when they're in business. "You can't do that," he insisted. "You can't afford to fool yourself—or Debbie."

Ray had set my mind whirling! I tossed the question over and over—and ultimately concluded that, yes, I am the same person and, yes, I *still* want to get married. There remained one reservation: my age. If I had been 25 instead of 20, I wouldn't have hesitated and I wouldn't have had doubts. But friends kept telling me that I was still too young to marry. I told them, I'm young chronologically, but I'm an adult emotionally. To me that's more significant.

During Christmas week 1973, I phoned Debbie from Detroit. Throughout the first half of the season I had felt a tremendous void, living on Long Island and not having Debbie around. There were women, sure, but I missed *Debbie*. There was no doubt in her mind that we should get married.

When the club flew to Montreal I picked out a diamond ring for her, had it cut specially and arranged, without her knowledge. I wanted very much to surprise Debbie with the ring. When the work had been completed, I invited her, her parents, and my folks to Montreal to see an Islanders game. I didn't say a word about the ring.

On the morning before the game the group of us took a walk through a large shopping center directly across the street from Montreal's Forum. I slowed our pace to allow my parents and relatives to move ahead of us. When we'd fallen far enough behind the old folks I handed Debbie the ring and we embraced in the middle of the shopping throng. Meanwhile, my parents thought they had lost us. We met them at a bar. My mother noticed the ring on Debbie's finger and asked about it. "Guess what," I said, "Debbie and I are engaged!"

Debbie had one reaction that really touched me. She was happy that I'd actually picked out the ring myself rather than handing her the money and asking her to buy it herself, as so many young husbands-to-be do today.

We arranged to be married in June 1974, but there was still a major problem, for Debbie was Protestant and I'm Catholic. I couldn't ask her to convert to my religion; but I certainly would have preferred that she did, and I told her so. Debbie decided to become a Catholic and her parents agreed.

A few weeks later I asked her how she felt about conversion. "If I'm going to give you my life as your wife, I'm prepared to give up my religion."

I was delighted—even more so because her parents encouraged Debbie to convert. I contacted an old confidant of mine, Father Fournier, who agreed to perform the conversion ceremony. By coincidence it was held on the Sunday morning that I learned I had won the Calder Trophy.

Between the celebration of my winning the rookie award and Debbie's conversion, we were up on Cloud 9 very early that Sunday—perhaps too early. We still had some important plans to complete (some rather bizarre moves, at that).

We had decided to rent a mobile home, a Winnebago, and drive it across the continent once all my hockey obligations were over. The problem was that we were in Ottawa and the Winnebago was waiting for us in New York. That meant we had to fly from Ottawa to New York, drive the big thing back to Ottawa, and then go on to Montreal in time for the awards. Well, we got to New York in time, but the ride back to Ottawa was very nearly the last ride Debbie and I ever took.

The Winnebago was a huge, van-like vehicle that had all the necessities of home as well as the appurtenances of a car. All but one—brakes. Almost from the moment we got the camper on the road, I found that it was difficult to stop. We took the New York State Thruway north toward Albany, and whenever I tried to slow down for a toll booth or a car, the camper acted like a tank. I figured this must be normal for a big truck like this. So I concentrated on keeping the camper at a safe distance from the other vehicles on the Thruway. But, as always, cars were cutting in and out and the journey got hairier and hairier as we approached Albany. Worse, the rain fell in torrents from the time we left New York City until we reached Canada. The windshield wipers stopped working altogether, and it was impossible to see clearly for more than a few yards.

How we did it I'll never know for sure, but we finally got the Winnebago to Ottawa. I was about ten pounds lighter after the ordeal. The first thing I did was to take the camper to our local auto mechanic and tell him to fix the windshield wipers.

The mechanic was fascinated with the Winnebago and eyed it from front to back, from top to bottom. I was hanging around just to get his verdict on the windshield wipers when he began probing around the rear axle.

"Hey, Denis," he screamed, "how far have you driven this lemon?"

"I took Route 87 from New York to Montreal and then 40 here from Montreal."

He crawled out from underneath the chassis and shook his head. "You're lucky you're alive. Look." He pointed to the brake drum under the car. Liquid was seeping out of the drum, and that meant only one thing: We had come as close to killing ourselves as we ever will. Just the thought of what I had done put a terrific scare in me. We had driven ten hours with my brakes failing!

I couldn't wait to get to Montreal, if only to take my mind off the near-disaster. I left almost immediately for the NHL awards banquet at the Bonaventure Hotel.

This should have been one of the high points in my life. Not only was I to receive the Calder Trophy, but I'd be standing alongside such superstars as Bobby Orr, Bernie Parent, and Johnny Bucyk, each of whom was in line for an award. But none of them appeared, and I was terribly disappointed that they took such a casual view of such an important ceremony for the hockey world. The only player who had a decent excuse was Orr. He said he couldn't make it because his wife was expecting their first baby. Bernie Parent was fishing and Johnny Bucyk had some other excuse. Their alibis didn't sound right to me.

My heart was throbbing when I was called on stage to receive the trophy from Syl Apps, the star center of the Toronto Maple Leafs in the late thirties and forties who was himself once a Calder Trophy winner. (His son now plays center for the Pittsburgh Penguins.)

It would be nice to say that I had been the unanimous choice as the NHL's best rookie, but that would be somewhat short of the truth. King Clancy, vice president of the Maple Leafs and an old Ottawa boy himself, went on record saying that he thought Toronto's rookie defenseman Borje Salming was "head and shoulders over Potvin defensively."

Clancy's observation didn't bother me half as much as some of the remarks made by the guy I had beaten out for the top spot, Tom Lysiak of Atlanta. Apparently he resented the fact that I had come out on top.

"Denis got all the write-ups in the magazines and newspapers, and there were five of us rookies who deserved just as much," Lysiak told magazine writer Jon Trontz. "I never saw stories about myself. It was all Potvin this, and Potvin that. Everywhere I went I heard his name. But since he got all the publicity, I figured he was another Orr. I just had to figure that he had it wrapped up from opening day. I thought he was going to be great. But you don't need great eyesight to see that Denis Potvin isn't Orr, or a great hockey player. Denis is a fancy talker. I might not talk as fancy. But he hasn't done anything on the ice."

I wasn't altogether surprised by Lysiak's remarks; I figured that, in my position, I'd just have to learn to expect some criticism. I won. He lost.

# 12

# THE ISLANDERS, THE COACH, AND ME

Midway in the 1975–76 season *The Toronto Star* sports page conducted an elaborate poll of NHL players to produce an offbeat All-Star Team. It included such categories ignored by the traditional All-Star selectors (the writers) as Best Face-Off Man and Fastest Skater. One category, Best NHL Coach, proved very startling with its result.

Nearly everybody assumed that the choice would be Freddie Shero, who had coached the Philadelphia Flyers to two consecutive Stanley Cup championships and had received more ink than nearly all the other NHL coaches combined. But Shero was bypassed in favor of the Islanders' pride and joy, Alger "Al" Arbour.

The surprise was understandable; Al is somewhat less than flamboyant. He rarely stirs the media because he sidesteps controversy, and he generally keeps a low profile, speaking softly but carrying an awfully big stick.

If Arbour and I had failed to hit it off in my rookie season, there never would have been a Calder Trophy—or any other NHL silverware—on my mantlepiece. Like any coach, he had make-or-break potential, and I knew from the start that he was the best possible mentor for me. Al's background told it all.

He had played 12 NHL seasons, alternately with Detroit, Chicago, Toronto, and St. Louis, and he had earned a reputation as a "defenseman's defenseman." That means that he was willing to be the foot soldier, doing the hard, heavy work in front of the net, in the corners, and along the boards, without concerning himself with goals or headlines. He was one of the few NHL defensemen ever to wear regular eyeglasses while playing, yet he thought nothing of hurling himself in front of 100-mile-per-hour shots if he thought he could prevent a goal. Knowing Al's background and appreciating the firm but helpful manner in which he dealt with me in my rookie year, I came to respect him more than any coach for whom I've played—and that in spite of my having become a big Leo Boivin fan in my last year with the Ottawa 67s.

A tall, lean man with an almost impassive expansion 99 percent of the time, Al established an unequivocal authority on the team. This was obvious in the players' behavior; almost to a man, nobody on the Islanders dares get snotty with the coach because the other players will immediately turn on the guy.

Inevitably, there are exceptions to the rule. These are the high-strung guys who may challenge Al on a point during a meeting. Once Al pointed out a flaw in one such guy's play and the player gave Al an argument while the rest of us just listened in disgust. We all knew the player was wrong and the coach was right. Al wasn't angry with the player; he let him make his point, then walked out of the room—and that was that.

If the club's situation goes beyond a one- or two-game losing streak, Al simply will not smile. (When he went three weeks once without smiling at anyone, we knew we had to do *something!* Captain Eddie Westfall called a private players' meeting—and that was really unusual for us since Al is the only guy wearing the stripes on the club.)

There's no support on the team for anyone who tries to get back at Al because, essentially, he's just voicing the thoughts of everyone on the team. Few coaches are more revered in any sport than Al is by the Islanders. And, as we were to discover during the 1975 Stanley Cup playoffs, there are few coaches more dedicated to his team than Al Arbour.

During the 1975 series against Pittsburgh, Al suddenly came up lame with severe back problems. As we fell behind the Penguins, one, two, three games, Al was in and out of the hospital, in and out of traction, and feeling very depressed because, *he* thought, he wasn't contributing enough to the club.

Following the third loss to Pittsburgh, Arbour left the hospital and met with us in the Islanders' dressing room. It was the most poignant scene I experenced since I had sat down with Dad after running away from home during my junior days. But this time the context was different.

Al, an imposing man with a dignity rarely seen in sports, greeted us and said: "Men, I have to apologize to you for not being able to coach you in the manner that I'd like. As you know, the back has been giving me a lot of problems and I feel that I owe you at least an apology for not doing more for you all."

The room was so quiet you could hear an ant breathe. To a man, the team was moved that Al would shoulder the blame (when he was blameless) for our being down three games with the Penguins.

Never in my playing career have I seen a team so galvanized to combat. Every Islander felt that he would personally plunge through the wall if it meant winning the series for the coach and removing any feeling of guilt he might have been suffering. That brief moment in the dressing room proved to be the turning point of the series. The Islanders were a "new" club after that, beating the Penguins in four straight games.

Thankfully, Al recovered from his back woes and has since been, literally, a pillar of strength for the club.

You can't try Al too much on anything, least of all the team rules. He has established a firm set of rules that are respected by the men. His entire philosophy is that the Islanders are a team that functions on mutual trust. We'll walk into a hotel after the bus ride from the airport, and he'll tell us: "All right, guys, we've got a big game tomorrow night. You know you have to take care of yourselves, so be in your rooms at eleven o'clock." Nine times out of ten he won't check. (But there's the odd time he will check, and if someone's missing, Al will fine him $500.)

But it's relatively painless to be fined; all that money goes into a separate account that we use at the end of the year for an enormous party for the players. Besides, the team often has a say in the nature and amount of a specific fine.

Once this year I was late for a practice, having been stopped by a policeman. Thinking I had a pretty good excuse, I strolled in waving the ticket I had been given. But Al just shrugged and said, "What can I do about it, Denis? You're late."

A bit later, Al came out on the ice and said, "All right, the court's in session. Denis, you're not part of it. Everyone else will judge the criminal" (meaning me). Under normal circumstances, I would have had to pay $100, because it was the second time I'd been late. (Each time a player's late, he pays double the amount he paid the time before. The first lateness costs $50.) But the players decided that there were extenuating circumstances and that I should be fined a token amount for being late. I paid $25.

That kind of trial doesn't happen all the time. Al doesn't use drastic punishments to get people to toe the line—he doesn't have to. We don't have any rebels on this club. When someone's done something, Al just strolls over and asks why. While the player explains, Al stands there with a little grin on his face. Then he ponders the fine. If, say, André St. Laurent is late, he'll put the whole line through our usual rink-length skate sprints, then he'll pull Howatt and Nystrom off and make Andy go back and forth four or five more times. Believe me, you'd rather pay up than go through that.

Because Al is the center of the team, and because we don't have any single "star," the team stays fairly close. Once in a while, somebody will point a finger and say, "You've been screwing up." Once in St. Louis, with us leading, 2–1, we were killing a penalty with about four minutes left in the game. I had the puck behind the net. Carrying the puck on my forehand, I looked up and saw Dave Lewis standing in front of the net and an opening on the other side. So I skated to the other side of the net, where I could fire the puck down the ice.

Just as I got there, Lewie moved over. I shot the puck and it hit him in the back of the leg, glanced off, and landed right on Red Berenson's backhand. Since Berenson has one of the better backhand shots in the league, I rushed out to try to stop his shot. Lewie did the same thing. But Berenson shot and the puck went past both of us and eluded goalie Chico Resch for the tying goal.

In the dressing room, Chico was upset. He thought both of us should have gone for the man in front of the net to give Chico a clear view of Berenson's shot. Lewie, Gerry Hart, and I all argued that Berenson, with his good backhand, was well inside the face-off circle, and that none of us would ever allow him to shoot from that close.

Jean joined in on our side, and Billy Smith on Chico's. The discussion became a bit acrimonious because all of us were trying to talk at once. Then Al came in, softly, careful not to disturb the argument. He waited, fully aware that sooner or later we'd ask his opinion.

We asked. Berenson, he replied, was indeed in a very dangerous spot, but the puck had gone off Claude Larose, who was standing in front of Chico, before it went into the net. One of us should have taken Larose out while the other went after Berenson. Neither I nor Lewie had seen Larose, so that settled matters right there.

Al has an even keener sense of what's happening on the ice. He knows the teams better than we do, so he's always having briefings. We have more meetings than any other club in the league. We average one in the morning before practice and another before the game, at about 6:45.

At the meetings, Al reviews his latest scouting reports and covers all bases. We go over the opposing team's style, how it's been playing of late, the goaltenders, the lines, the offensive threats, the weaknesses, even injuries. Generally, though, the morning meeting is devoted to the overall system of the team, the afternoon meeting to individual players.

During the playoffs, Al calls one more meeting, at 9:30 or 10:00 at night on a non-game night, just to make sure everyone's there. That is a pain in the neck. Everybody on the team, including me, thinks we have far too many meetings. But it's Al's way of keeping us disciplined.

We also keep disciplined by all the practices. The players don't mind them unless we're not clicking, because Al likes to see us look good even in practice. If we have a bad practice, we're sure to have a bad game because our practices are so tightly organized that we get into a trend. After two bad practices in a row, Al will stop the third if it gets off on the wrong foot and start all over again.

Nobody on this team would contradict Al, not even Eddie Westfall. Chico Resch might come close, but he'd think twice about it. Chico came up as a quiet guy who rarely questioned anybody, but since the 1976 playoffs he has said more about what he feels, especially to the press.

Sometimes he's misquoted in the newspapers, and this has caused some friction among the players. In this year's playoffs against Montreal, Chico was discouraged because he thought we could have put up a better effort. He spoke to Tim Moriarty of *Newsday* about it, and the next day Moriarity had an article in the paper suggesting that Resch thought the team might have quit.

As soon as the players saw the article, they started making little digs at Chico. Most of us like to think the Islanders have a reputation of not being quitters, and some of the guys, including Al, didn't like the article one bit. Al even went around asking if any of us had spoken to Moriarty. Then he called a special meeting and said, "Nobody on this team is a quitter. If anybody on this team quits, they're gone."

Meanwhile, Chico was very upset. He told us he had only said we "could have played better." Chico was visibly hurt because he implicitly believes in the unity of our club. Chico's a great competitor. But he has to be cocky, sure of himself, to succeed. He's one of the most popular guys on the team, but, after all, he's a goaltender, and they're all "different."

The Islanders' goalies stick together. Reporters don't understand that. If Chico has been playing awhile, the press will automatically go to Smitty and expect him to say something unfavorable about Chico—

which never happens because they're as close as any two guys on the team. Besides, Smitty is sharp and funny and easy to get along with.

We rarely have real fights. There's a time for each player when he's not in the mood for clubhouse clowning. Take, for instance, my brother Jean. He's the type who's always telling jokes, funny or otherwise. If a joke he tells isn't funny, he laughs enough for everybody. But some mornings Jean comes in, walks to his locker, sits down, and doesn't say anything. If he hasn't said anything by the time he gets to his locker, we all know he's not in a good mood. So we leave him alone.

It doesn't take long for a player's personal radar to tell him which teammates to fool with and which to leave alone. You never question goalies; they are a breed apart and everybody knows that. Billy and Chico have always been very much into themselves, and when the club is on the road, they will invariably take off together to eat, then return to the hotel and watch television all night. Others, like Jean, Jude Drouin, and André St. Laurent, usually go out for a few drinks after we check into our hotel.

Bert Marshall and Gerry Hart are among the quieter and moodier guys in the dressing room. It's not unusual for Bert to walk into the dressing room with a snarl to make your blood curdle—if you take it seriously. We don't, and when Bert is in a punko mood we needle the pants off him until he winds up screaming and cursing at us. It's great for an early morning laugh—or a fight.

A guaranteed fight-producer is that grisly hockey tradition known as "The Shave," with which I had a brief encounter when I played for Ottawa. For years The Shave has been a ritual to be inflicted on NHL rookies.

By far the worst shave I ever saw inflicted was one we gave to one of my teammates. Not only did he get shaved, but after the ritual we strapped him to a chair and tied a string around his penis. One of the guys held the string so that when he moved, the string pulled tighter. We finally let him go and ran like hell. The guy came storming after us, screaming threats that would curdle milk. Luckily, none of my buddies got caught and, as usually happens after a shave, the victim cooled down.

Not everybody would get the de luxe treatment we provided for this particular individual. We couldn't pull pranks like that on everyone.

Garry Howatt starts a lot of the dressing room shenanigans. He is a relatively small guy who burns up tremendous amounts of energy and he likes to take out some of his aggression on his teammates, in a harmless way. Garry likes to go up to big guys like Bobby Nystrom and Clark Gillies and slap them in the face: the classic introduction to a fight—which is just what Garry wants.

Clark will usually just push him away and try not to be bothered, but Garry has a way of persisting and, pretty soon, they'll wind up on the floor in a wrestling match, like kids in a sandbox. You feel like you're at ringside. It's difficult to avoid Garry because he's such an intense guy, even when he's fooling around. When he wrestles, his veins stick out of his skin as if he's fighting for his life—which, in a way, he is.

It's impossible to shave Garry. Most other guys are "shavable," but every so often events of the moment force us to cancel our plans. That happened in the middle of the 1975–76 season. We wanted to get Bryan Trottier, our bashful rookie who went on to win the Calder Trophy. The idea was to get Bryan at the end of our West Coast trip, after we had played Vancouver, Oakland, and Los Angeles. But Bryan escaped because by the time we had left L. A. we had lost three straight games. The guys were too depressed even to pick up a razor.

There are few athletes in or out of hockey whom I respect more than Garry Howatt, the Islanders forward we call The Toy Tiger. Garry is living proof that a hockey player with minimal skills can be a successful major leaguer if he works his butt off, keeps practicing, and gives 150 percent in games. And he's managed to become an effective scoring threat and a solid two-way player while conquering epilepsy.

Garry and I both arrived on the Islanders with reputations as tough guys. But, apart from a few innocuous flare-ups, nothing much ever happened between Howatt and me. Garry once told me, "Y'know, Denis, I thought I'd be competing with you in the fight department and that you and I would go at it a lot. Now, we're the best of friends."

One aspect of the professional hockey player's life often overlooked by the average fan is the relationship that teammates develop simply by being thrown together as roommates on the road. On our club, Al Arbour maintains a rigid policy of rooming defensemen with defensemen, forwards with forwards, and goalies with goalies, no doubt on the assumption that in this way roommates will have more in common with one another.

I've had only two roommates since I've been with the Islanders: Gerry Hart and Dave Fortier. My relationship with each has become deeper, if not closer—especially with Hart, since Gerry and I have roomed together the longest. It has been a fortuitous coupling of personalities for me. Gerry is a lot like myself; he does a lot of thinking and he understands me more than the rest of the guys do. Gerry also happens to be a great guy, which helps.

Understanding each other's individual idiosyncrasies is perhaps the most significant factor in the success of teammates rooming together. Gerry, for example, knows that when I sit down to read a book, I don't want to be hassled. Likewise, I am aware of his little quirks. I've come to live with the fact that Gerry will spend hours in the bathtub but won't allow the television to be on when he falls asleep. So I forsake late night TV when I'm with Hart, and I read a book.

If that sounds as though it takes an effort to make a success of a roommate relationship, imagine how much work goes into keeping harmony on a team with 18 differing personalities and backgrounds, a team where you have such diverse individuals as a French-Canadian like me from Ottawa, an English-Canadian like Billy Harris from a metropolis like Toronto, and a part French, part Indian, part English-Canadian like Bryan Trottier, who grew up on a farm in a remote town called Val Marie, Saskatchewan.

Looking at the Islanders from another point of view, you'll find myself, my brother, Eddie Westfall, Jude Drouin, André St. Laurent, and Ralph Stewart, who enjoy dropping in to a tavern for a beer when we're on the road. Gerry Hart is a little more particular; he favors a cocktail lounge and won't always take off with us beer-drinkers. Then you have the seven or eight guys like Bryan Trottier who don't drink at all, and whom you never see out on the town because they go their own individual ways, usually shopping, on the day of a game.

Still another strata, a more subtle but still distinct classification, is based on prestige. It is something clearly defined only by the bench-warmer himself, something that sets the regular apart from the part-time player.

Lorne Henning was a perfect example of that type of individual who was not a member of the "upper class" of regulars during my first two years with the Islanders. Lorne, who is one of the best guys you'll meet anywhere, anytime, was one of the original Islanders who suffered so much in the first two difficult years when losing had been a way of life.

He was sent to the American League (New Haven) in 1972–73 and to the Central League (Fort Worth) in 1974–75, and he must have suffered serious doubts about his ability to stick in the big leagues. When he returned to our club in the 1974–75 season, Lorne betrayed the typical introversion of a non-regular: He was more quiet than the guys who were taking a regular turn on the ice. It was a natural reaction. When a guy plays regularly, he participates more and he senses this. The guy who warms the bench is like an injured player. He doesn't feel a *part* of the team.

In Henning's case the happy turnabout occurred in the 1975–76 season when he blossomed into one of the best—if not *the* best— penalty-killers in the NHL and a superb defensive forward with marvelous insight into the game itself. At precisely the time that the fans and the press began appreciating him, Lorne emerged from his shell. He realized that he was not on the trading block, that he was a valuable cog in the Islanders' machine, and that the fans had come to dig his talents.

Still another distinction must be made between the practice-lovers such as Bert Marshall, who wants everyone to work hard even in scrimmages (and who is extremely intense about the game) and the practice-haters like lazy Denis Potvin.

Along with Eddie Westfall and J. P. Parise, I get on the ice at 11 A.M. when practice begins and I'm off the ice punctually the moment practice ends. Then there are guys like Garry Howatt, who will lift weights and punch the bag for 20 minutes in the exercise room after practice. People like myself get out as quickly as they can on the theory that it's important to think about things *other* than hockey. If I get too involved, it's simply not good for my head.

At times I feel in my head that I'm the black sheep, or the ugly duckling, of the Islanders. It turned out that the ugly duckling wasn't *really* ugly after all, and I like to think that I could be as much liked by my teammates as anyone else in the dressing room. But this just isn't the case, and it can be very depressing for me.

I'm always reminded of what Billy Harris once told me: "Denis, everybody likes you, but nobody knows where you're at!"

Well, *I* know where I'm at; what bothers me is that I can't get that through to anybody else. I *am* different from the other hockey players. When I talk about my love of art, about Debbie and me taking trips to the Guggenheim Museum in Manhattan, the other players say, "What the hell is this guy all about?"

In turn, I become self-conscious because I know that I don't think and act like the average hockey player and I get criticized for it. Not that the criticism is open and direct; it happens in an oblique way. Take the phone calls from my teammates. On the road, I'll never be asked by the guys to go out and have a few laughs. Yet an extrovert like Chico Resch will get two or three calls from different players.

Sometimes I have the feeling that if it weren't for my brother's being on the team, I'd never go out when we're on the road, I'd just hole myself up in the room and read.

Yet I love the Islanders; there isn't a single guy on our team I wouldn't defend in *any* situation, in a bar, in a game, or in print. If there's a hassle on the ice with a little guy like André St. Laurent, who can usually take care of himself, I'll be the first one to help him if he's getting the worst of it.

I know the players themselves are aware that I'll react this way to them, yet I'll say to myself, Sonofabitch, Denis, you're damned popular but nobody on the team likes you!

I'd dearly love to have my teammates come over and give me a little advice: Denis, you're not passing the puck quickly enough; or Denis, you're not using your body to advantage, maybe you should try it this way.

Al Arbour and Bill Torrey are the only ones who seem to communicate with me—and maybe it's because we talk on the same level.

This, obviously, will give the impression that I'm isolated from my teammates. In the latter part of the 1975–76 season, I had the opportunity to learn whether or not this was the case when Debbie and I were chairpersons of an Easter Seals dinner to which all of the Islanders players were invited. For me this would be a quiet test of how the guys felt about me—and about a good cause.

Every single player on the team showed up (with one exception, who had a good excuse), and everyone reacted with such enthusiasm and class that I was never so touched in my life. It wasn't just that they gave themselves, but after it was over the players came over to me and said, "Denis, that was great; you can be sure we'll be here next year."

If nothing else, it proved that I wasn't an ugly duckling after all.

# 13

# THEY SAID IT COULDN'T BE DONE, AND OTHER REMINDERS OF THE 1942 MAPLE LEAFS

Part of the competitive excitement of hockey is the blossoming of a rivalry. Long before the Islanders and the Rangers started getting mad at each other there were some wonderfully nerve-tingling battles. In Montreal, the Canadiens (representing the French-speaking population) used to go at it hammer and tongs with the Maroons (who carried the banner for English-speaking Quebec). Their counterparts in New York City were the Americans and the Rangers.

The Americans aren't around anymore, but they were the first NHL team in town; in fact, they opened Madison Square Garden in 1925. The Rangers came a year later, and pretty soon half of New York was rooting for the Amerks and the other half was cheering for the Blue-shirts. That rivalry peaked just before the start of World War II, when the great Eddie Shore finished his NHL career with the Americans and Ching Johnson was doling out bodychecks for the Rangers.

The Americans were a hard-luck team and, by 1942, their luck had run out, along with their money. When they could no longer pay their bills, Madison Square Garden closed its doors on them and the Rangers had the ice to themselves forever—or so it seemed then; in time, NHL expansion changed all that. When the Coliseum in Uniondale, Long Island, was built it was inevitable that the New York metropolitan area would soon have another big-league team. In 1972 the Islanders were born.

Their first year in the NHL, 1972–73, was an artistic failure like the league had never known before. Worse, the Rangers lorded it over the Islanders, not only beating the expansion baby but in the case of several Rangers, treating the Islanders with a contempt that surpassed even humiliation. When I joined the team for the 1973–74 season, teammates Eddie Westfall and Billy Harris had a lot to say about the guff the

Islanders had had to take from the Pete Stemkowskis, Brad Parks, and other Rangers.

Anyone who loved an underdog wound up rooting for us, and by the start of the 1974–75 season our rivalry had simmered to the boiling point and was becoming still hotter by the month. One of the reasons for the antagonism, naturally, was the amount of press coverage we got every time we played the Rangers. "Their games," said Tim Moriarty of *Newsday,* "have developed intense fan interest, especially now that the clubs are playing in the same division."

Adding to the rivalry was my winning the Calder Trophy and the challenge I presented to Brad Park. "Like Ching Johnson and Eddie Shore before them," wrote Moriarty, "Park and Potvin rank as the top defensemen in the NHL."

From what I gathered, Park had owned New York before I came along. By January 1975 that had changed; I was playing well enough for *Newsday* to run a major feature, WHO'S BETTER, POTVIN OR PARK?

As you'd expect, those who were surveyed divided along partisan lines. Al Arbour voted for me. "I have to give Denis the edge over Park," said Al, "because of what he's contributing to our club. He's been a tremendous asset."

Rangers coach Emile Francis voted for Park (I can't blame him for that). One of the most interesting comments came from my teammate, Bert Marshall, who had played for the Rangers—and with Park—before coming to the Islanders. "Brad and Denis have different styles," said Marshall, who knows his defense. "There are times when Brad can take more chances because he feels there will be somebody there to back him up. Denis can't do that for fear of losing the puck. But I like Denis' approach to the game. He keeps insisting he doesn't want to be the second Bobby Orr but the first Denis Potvin. And I tend to agree with him."

Park himself had this to say: "We're different hockey players and hard to compare. It's like comparing me with Orr. What you're dealing with here are offensive defensemen who can handle the puck. In that respect, I think Denis does it very well."

By the time the season had ended, there wasn't much doubt that I had caught up to Park. I had been named to the First All-Star Team; Park hadn't. Being compared to Orr was an honor, but by this time I was contributing more than Park.

As for Orr, I knew it would be hard to dislodge him from the Norris

Trophy for the best NHL defenseman because he scores so many points. But his point total alone didn't mean that he was best. I refused to agree that Orr at his best contributed more to his club than I—or that he was the best ever. Sure, Orr changed the game, but I'm for more positional play. I knew that I didn't have his spectacular style and that I wasn't as good a skater, but that didn't mean much to me. I had developed a fanatical obsession about being the best; I *had* to be the best.

In April 1975 the Islanders helped me take a step in that direction. Playing in the Lester Patrick Division of the NHL meant that we had to beat out the Atlanta Flames if we were going to make the Stanley Cup playoffs along with the Rangers and the Flyers.

It was touch and go between us and Atlanta in the last weeks of March, but we had gotten a tremendous break when manager Bill Torrey obtained Jude Drouin and J. P. Parise from the Minnesota North Stars just before the trade deadline. Jude and "Jeep" gave us the extra scoring punch we needed, and for the first time the Islanders were in the playoffs.

As if Hollywood were scripting the scenario, our first-round opponents were the Rangers—who, by this time, had become affectionately known as "the hated" Rangers. Since this was the opening round, it would be only a best-of-three series with games one and three (if necessary) at Madison Square Garden and the second game at our home rink, Nassau Coliseum.

We thought the Rangers would be an extremely difficult opponent with Stanley Cup veterans like Rod Gilbert, Eddie Giacomin, and Jean Ratelle. The Rangers also had a smart coach in Emile Francis. And they were a fairly big club, with guys like Pete Stemkowski, Jerry Butler, Ted Irvine, and my favorite foe, Brad Park. But for some reason—maybe not the decisive one—they were a club that we knew could be pushed around and even intimidated if we manhandled them in the right way.

There seemed to me to be a definite pattern for the care and mishandling of a Ranger player. They were called "fat cats" for a very good reason: Madison Square Garden was paying them more money, as a team, than any other NHL club, yet they gave little in return. The obvious conclusion, to me, was that the Rangers played for the money and nothing else. The typical Ranger seemed to be a skater who lacked drive, who missed the extra step necessary for victory. Everybody on that club seemed to diddle-daddle a lot and become depressed easily if the puck didn't bounce their way.

The Rangers had *always* seemed to be this way, as far back as I can remember. As a kid following hockey, I felt that the Canadiens were the prideful club of the NHL, the one with the rich tradition and the will to give their all for the glory of French Canada. The Rangers never showed me that extra tenaciousness that the Canadiens or the Bruins have always had. They didn't have the mean streak that would make them want to beat an enemy badly or make them come from behind when they were down by three or four goals.

Pinpointing a problem like that isn't easy; but one factor had been constant with the Rangers for as long as I could remember: Emile Francis. More often than not, he had held the jobs of both general manager and coach of the Rangers—which I think is the problem. A manager must keep his distance from the players. He's the guy who negotiates contracts, makes trades, and handles other affairs that frequently inspire the anger of players. The coach, by contrast, should be a close, father-like figure. The two functions rarely meld well together. Francis coached and managed the Rangers from 1964 through 1976 and never won a championship.

Our strategy for preventing their doing it in 1975 revolved around a few basic strategies. One was to outhustle and outhit them; another involved outflanking their "wandering" goalie, Ed Giacomin. Like Jacques Plante, who developed the practice of skating behind his net to field the puck, Giacomin was an excellent skater for a goalie and a splendid stickhandler. He was virtually a third defenseman for the Rangers. He would skate way out of his crease if he saw the puck skimming along the boards near the net, trap the puck and attempt a forward pass to one of his teammates who then would counterattack. Our plan was to dump the puck into the corner and make Giacomin wander after it and then try to intercept his clearing passes. Better still, if we could get to the puck before Giacomin, there was an outside chance that one of the Islanders could come around and stuff the rubber into the open Ranger net.

Coach Arbour's best-laid plans fell to pieces in the first two periods of the first game. We gave up a pair of goals in the second period, and while we sat in the dressing room before the third period Eddie Westfall sensed that the younger players on the club needed a good shot of confidence. So he went around the room boosting all the kids: "All we need," he told us, "is one goal, and we'll be okay."

Eddie had a calming effect on the gang, and within five minutes of the third period we finally put the light on behind Giacomin. Billy Harris did the trick after Parise and Drouin—I told you that was a heckuva trade—had passed the puck around Giacomin's cage on a power play.

That was especially gratifying because until then the highfalutin' Rangers had been making fun of our power play, and it made our guys good and mad. I'm sure it forced us to work harder. Just as Eddie Westfall had said, the goal suddenly made everything okay for us. We reversed the pressure on the Rangers and began using the "dump the puck" plan until it finally worked.

Jean was the guy who made it all possible, after Billy MacMillan had followed the blueprint and shot the puck into Giacomin's end on a perfect angle. Giacomin started on his usual wandering act, but Jean outraced him, flipped the puck over Giacomin's stick, and controlled it behind the net. By now Giacomin was in the far corner and Jean had a chance to swerve quickly and go for the opening.

"I saw the wide-open net," he told me later, "and I got a little jittery. It looked so gorgeous. So I came around the left post and made absolutely sure." That he did, and it was now a 2–2 hockey game. The Rangers were on the ropes.

Some critics have said that the Islanders were too young to develop a blood lust for the enemy's jugular when we had them in trouble. That may have been true in certain situations, but it wasn't true when we were up against the Rangers. We knew they were staggering and we knew they couldn't cope well with adversity. A few minutes later we proved it when big rookie Clark Gillies took a pass from Westfall at the blue line and smashed past defensemen Gilles Marotte and Ron Greschner. When he was 15 feet from Giacomin, Clark pulled the trigger and we were ahead, 3–2.

That did it. Our goalie Glenn Resch held on and we finished with what the local writers called an upset. Now the Islanders were the toast of New York. *The Post* described us as "the never-say-die Islanders." Jack Chevalier in *The Philadelphia Bulletin* had an even better line: "The Islanders proved that wet-behind-the-ears is a better condition than egg-on-the-face."

Even the Rangers acknowledged our desire, for a change. "We had them," said Ted Irvine, "but we let up and they wouldn't quit." Ron Greschner, the young Ranger defenseman, promised they'd stuff it down our throats in the second game. And he was right.

Everything that could possibly go wrong, from lousy refereeing to endless fighting, occurred in the game we had hoped would be the clincher before our home fans. We got bombed, 8–3, and the less said about the debacle the better. It only set us up for a showdown and a test of whether we qualified under the bromide, "When the going gets tough, the tough get going!"

It got tough for us on April 11, 1975, at Madison Square Garden. For beating the Rangers on their home ice in the final game of a playoff round was generally considered a bit much for the Islanders at that point. But those inside our dressing room had different thoughts.

I remembered what Billy MacMillan had said at breakfast in Atlanta a week before the regular season had ended. "We'll make the playoffs," he said, "and once we're in, our horizons will be unlimited."

At a team meeting late in the season J. P. Parise had told us that every team in the league had a lot of respect for the Islanders. "You guys don't seem to realize how good you are," Parise said. That was important because J. P. had seen us from another perspective—he had played against us most of the season.

A lot of us remembered what Parise had said. We told ourselves, Hey, if we're that good, let's see what we can do about it. When we stepped out on Madison Square Garden ice for the third and final game against the Rangers we *were* believing in ourselves.

I'm not sure what the Rangers were thinking. I know they had been antagonized by Islanders fans at the Coliseum, for CHOKE signs were all over the place and they were directed at one team—the Rangers.

For two periods it appeared as if the Rangers had caved in. Clark Gillies put us ahead by one in the first period and then I got two in the second. We opened the third period with an unbelievable three-goal lead. Al Arbour had taken a gamble and put Billy Smith in the nets for Resch, who had gotten bombed at the Coliseum. Billy was tremendous.

But at 4:44 of the third period Billy Fairbairn beat him and then at 13:27 Fairbairn did it again and, all of a sudden, we were playing like a bunch of schoolkids. If you had told me that the Garden rink was tilted 80 degrees downhill against us I would have believed it. Steve Vickers tied the game at 13:41 and we all seemed tired. But all of us were aware of the consequences if we gave up then, so we dug in, and we held on until the period ended.

The score now was 3–3 and the game would be settled in the most pulsating and excruciating manner of all, sudden-death overtime. Many of us suffered self-doubt in those moments before we took the ice again for the most decisive 11 seconds of our lives. Even hardbitten veterans such as Bert Marshall were worried. "It's an inner thing," was the way

Bert put it later. "There was some fear on the club. But we had to realize that *everybody* has self-doubts on occasions. Maybe the Rangers were worried that things wouldn't work out for them. Our secret was to control those fears, to channel them so that they can make us better."

We started with the face-off at center ice. Jude Drouin was up front with Eddie Westfall and J. P. Parise. They had in mind a play that often worked: When Jude gets the puck in the corner, J. P. will go behind the net, and they'll pass it around until they think they can make a play on goal. This time they made a slight variation on it.

We got the puck into the Rangers' zone and for a moment it looked like Steve Vickers would be able to clear it out of danger, but Vickers missed the puck and Jude got his stick on it. Instead of going behind the net for Drouin's usual pass, Parise took a gamble and parked in front of Giacomin, mostly because nobody checked him (the guy who *should* have been doing it was Brad Park). Drouin didn't make a normal pass; he took what amounted to a compressed slapshot toward the goal, hoping it might go in if Parise didn't reach it.

Park realized he had left J. P. uncovered and tried to tie him up just as the puck arrived at Giacomin's doorstep. The Ranger goalie saw imminent doom and tried to head it off by using his goal stick, but the puck was moving too fast. J. P. planted his stick in front of the rubber and the next thing we knew the red light was on and all hell was breaking loose among the guys in the dark jerseys. At 11 seconds of the overtime period, we not only knocked out the Rangers but set a playoff record. We now owned New York.

"As I was saying," said Billy MacMillan, "our horizons are unlimited."

Less than an hour after we had pulled off one of the biggest upsets in sports history, we were being badmouthed by the Rangers. The highest decibel count in the losers' dressing room came from Derek Sanderson, author, bon vivant, and general provocateur.

"The Atlanta Flames are better than the Islanders," snapped Sanderson before the Rangers' dead body had cooled. "The Islanders won't win another playoff game."

My teammates weren't amused to hear of Sanderson's remark—until J. P. provided the last word: "I don't know about us, but I can guarantee that the Rangers won't win another playoff game this season!" That broke up the room.

Sanderson wasn't the only Ranger to get our goat. Steve Vickers was quoted as saying, "It's the most embarrassing defeat I've ever suffered, losing to the Islanders . . ."

In Pittsburgh, the Penguins were waiting to start the best-of-seven semi-final against us. Vic Hadfield of the Penguins said it best: "We seem to have a lot in common with the Islanders. They have some young fellows and other guys with a lot of experience and so do we. It figures to be a tough series and I wouldn't be surprised if it goes seven games."

Beating the Rangers had been a matter of pride; facing the Penguins was more a competition, a challenge. It was pure playoff hockey, and in the opener we were beaten, 5–4, by a hot goalie, Gary Inness. Every time we shot, Inness seemed to come up with the save. Strangely, our scouting report had said he was weak on high shots, low shots, rebounds, and covering up on his angles. You couldn't tell it from our performance.

Inness was even better in the second game. With 40 seconds left in the second period, he stopped Bobby Nystrom right in front of the net and they went on to take us, 3–1. On top of that, I had aggravated a pulled groin muscle on my left side, which had limited my skating by 40 percent.

Fans often hear the expression "pulled muscle" but they have no idea what a painful experience it is for the athlete. In this case I had to favor the entire leg for the full 60 minutes of the game. I couldn't dig my skates into the ice for quick bursts, and I had no strength in my stride when I pushed off. The quick burst coming out of our end wasn't there. I couldn't afford to go in too deep because I knew I couldn't return to my defensive position fast enough. My leg felt like there was a knife in it.

I wasn't at all happy with my performance but, to my surprise, the Penguins were impressed. After the second game I picked up the papers —and there was Inness, of all people, talking about me the way I've talked about him: "Potvin didn't look restricted to me. He's super. Anytime he's on the ice there's danger for us. Everything about the Islanders revolves around him."

They could afford to be kind. Riding the wave of a two-game lead, the Penguins invaded our Coliseum and bombed us 6–4 in the third game and, just as I had feared, the writers dredged up Derek Sanderson's prophecy that we'd never win another playoff game.

With the exception of the 1942 Toronto Maple Leafs, no team in NHL history has rebounded from a no-games-to-three deficit in a best-of-seven series to win four straight. There was no reason, considering our efforts in the first three games with Pittsburgh, to think that we might enter the record books beside the storied Toronto team.

To say we had our doubts about taking Pittsburgh would be the understatement of the half-century. We skated onto the Nassau Coliseum ice just hoping to produce a solid effort for the 14,865 fans who gave us a standing ovation as we lined up for the pre-game practice. I looked up at the fans and there, plastered across the wall at the very top of the arena was a sign that read: MAPLE LEAFS 1942. It didn't require any explanation.

Three hours later, when we had skated off with a 3–1 victory, I thought about that sign again and about what Billy MacMillan had been saying all along: "It's a helluva way to play the game—facing adversity and then having to overcome it. But we always seem to reach our goal."

I wasn't so sure. Since the Ranger series I had taken 31 shots on goal without lighting a single red light against the Penguins. On their own ice for game five, they figured to be murder, so we planned accordingly: We switched airlines for the flight to Pittsburgh and when we arrived we checked into a hotel the club hadn't patronized in more than two years. "I'm not superstitious, but . . ." was Bill Torrey's explanation.

We weren't going to quarrel with that, as long as we survived to return to Pittsburgh for a seventh game. And we *didn't* quarrel, not after taking the Penguins, 4–2.

I could see the mistakes that we had been making in the first three losses now that they were no longer happening. We had been playing their game, letting them catch us down ice, then letting them throw two- and three-man breaks at us. What changed things was that we got our heads on right just in time and began playing our own tight brand of hockey. If we could stick to that style in the sixth game, at home, we'd take Pittsburgh in the seventh on their ice.

One of the many guys who was making the miracle possible was our handsome, single, free-swinging center Ralph Stewart. Although he didn't get much ice time, Stewie was always good for laughs. He was the kind of guy who would go into a night spot and hand to an attractive female a calling card which read:

> IF THERE'S ANY CHANCE
> OF US MAKING IT TONIGHT
> SMILE
> OTHERWISE TEAR THIS UP

The catch was that Stewie's card was made of some resilient material that would only bend or curl up, no matter how much pressure was applied to it. Something about the Islanders was reminiscent of the texture of that card. We would not be torn asunder by the Penguins, and we proved it in the sixth game when Stewie took a pass from me early in the second period and pumped a shot past Gary Inness for the game's first score. The Penguins did rally once—Pierre Larouche tied the score, 1–1—but later in the period Garry Howatt put us ahead to stay, and we added two more in the third period and trooped off with a 4–1 win.

I realize we sounded more immodest by the day, but our crusade was being articulated by the opposition as much as by our own people. "The Islanders will never quit," was the way Inness put it. "They work hard, they play good positional hockey; they have a good coach and good goaltending."

Our name was alternating from "Never-Say-Die Islanders" to "Miracle Islanders" and back again. Cartoonist Bill Gallo of the *Daily News* pictured us on a desert island with our hands outstretched as an ocean liner cruised by with the name USS Miracle painted on its hull. The Islanders were shouting to the world: "And who said I missed the boat!"

How did we get this far when we should have been dead at least a week or, if you believe the Rangers, a month?

The coach deserved as much of the credit as our manager, who swung the deal for J. P. and Jude, and the rank-and-file players themselves. Right from the start of game four with Pittsburgh, Arbour kept repeating: "We're goin' to play it *one period* at a time. Then, one game at a time." That bromidic brand of planning took us a long way.

The dirtiest word in hockey, C-H-O-K-E, didn't crop up in the Pittsburgh series until the night before the finale. Pierre Larouche, one of the brashest kids ever to hit the big time, was the guy who uttered it. "The last game," said Lucky Pierre, "is a goalie's game. If Gary chokes or Resch chokes, the other team's going to win."

Bert Marshall, typically, had the answer to Larouche. "When the kid says the goalie chokes, he'd better look elsewhere. He's really saying that somebody else made a mistake in front of the goalie."

Within 24 hours Larouche would eat his words. I wouldn't say that he choked, but if a goat had to be picked from among the Penguins, Unlucky Pierre would have to be the guy. It was a perfect 0–0 game in the third period when Larouche orbited into a breakaway that could have won the game for Pittsburgh. It was the classic hockey confrontation, the mongoose (goalie) vs. the cobra (shooter).

Resch would not be out-psyched by the kid. He made the decisive move, daringly skating right out to Pierre as Larouche prepared to shoot. Then Chico threw himself headfirst to the ice, nicking the puck with the tip of his stick and getting enough of it to deflect it harmlessly away. Chico had hermetically sealed his goal for the night.

Now it was our turn to test Gary Inness once more. Bert Marshall, who had become our supreme diagnostician, skimmed a pass to Eddie Westfall and our steady captain found the opening we had been looking for all night. His shot flipped over Inness at 14:42. Resch had locked up the game and thrown away the key and we leaped off the ice—after leaping all over each other—with a 1–0 win.

If our defeating the Rangers was a high, this was euphoria multiplied by 50. After the usual post-game madness we all repaired to the eighth floor of the Carlton House Hotel and laughed and drank and sang until it seemed the entire hotel was up with us. At 2:30 A.M. we suddenly remembered that we should call Derek Sanderson to remind him of his wonderful prediction after the Rangers' series. But dawn hadn't broken yet, so we figured Derek wouldn't be home.

The best line of all was delivered by our coach. Long after midnight, somebody heard him mutter, "I don't think I'll have a bed check tonight!"

Next thing I remember was sitting groggy-eyed in the hotel coffee shop. It was morning. A newspaperman walked over to my table and told me I looked as though I hadn't had much sleep. I couldn't resist the smile. I told him, "Nobody else in that hotel did either, I guess."

Our bus left for the Pittsburgh airport at 8:30 A.M. and, to tell you the truth, I expected a real hero's welcome when we returned to LaGuardia Airport. But there was only a handful there. When we arrived at the Coliseum in the team bus, we were met by the wives and girlfriends. Many of the women had brought bottles of champagne. One of them offered Al Arbour a drink but he politely declined. "I'll drink it," he said, "when we win the Stanley Cup."

Others couldn't wait. We toasted and drank and toasted again and drank some more until the realization set in that in a matter of hours we'd have to start preparing for the semi-finals against the Philadelphia Flyers, the defending world champions.

If it was possible to be troubled by anything in such a deliriously happy time, I was concerned about the image we were developing as "miracle workers." Wherever you turned, somebody was writing that we could do anything.

After our coach declined to sip champagne prematurely, *Newsday* columnist Ed Comerford made the typical remark: "Please don't say it can't be done," said Comerford. "This is a team that keeps doing things that everybody says can't be done."

Remarks such as these looked good in print, but if we had believed them we would have been overconfident at a time we could least afford that feeling. They were talking about us as if we were gods when we were just some 20 guys not wanting to quit the game at this time of year because the summer would be so long.

# 14

# AND THEN THERE WAS KATE SMITH

As stirring as our comeback against the Penguins had been, I knew in my bones that the semi-final match with Freddie Shero's Philadelphia Flyers would be about as easy as going for a swim in a meat grinder. Not only did we have to cope with the coaching machinations of Shero (at his best a combination of Machiavelli, Merlin, and Mahatma Gandhi) but there was also the matter of Bobby Clarke, Bill Barber, Dave Schultz, Bernie Parent, and, seemingly, a cast of thousands.

And *then* there was the awful knowledge that if we backed the Flyers into a *cul de sac,* they might sound the trumpets and bring up the most unique "reserve" in hockey, Kate Smith!

Some of our guys, especially Chico Resch, had been publicly critical of the Flyers' "style" of roughhouse play. I didn't share that opinion. Sure, Philadelphia's team has been called The Broad Street Bullies, The Ferocious Flyers, and The Mean Machine, but they didn't invent tough hockey. They were only forced to toughen up their roster after years of being pushed around by earlier "heavies" such as the big, bad Boston Bruins and the surly St. Louis Blues.

I enjoyed skating against the Flyers because they were a team that had players who took care of trouble when it erupted (so did we). More than that, I respected them for their "system." It is the kind of game plan which works so well that anyone who could skate in the NHL could play for the Flyers. Give a draft pick a season in Philadelphia and the kid will emerge a good hockey player; the proof is in guys like Don Saleski, Mel Bridgeman, and Orest Kindrachuk. None of them were especially gifted when they reached the Flyers, but all are playing a superior game of hockey now. One of the reasons for this is the discipline Shero instills in his team and which Captain Bobby Clarke enforces.

Clarke is an exceptionally deceptive hockey player. He gets lauded from here to Hong Kong because he *appears* to be working harder than any dozen other hockey players in the rink. The fact is, he takes two strides and assumes that desperate look of his because he's such a poor skater. In the same way, *appearance* hurts a player like myself. My skating style is more fluid and I don't give the idea that I'm busting my chops, but actually I'm working just as hard as Clarke at any given time. Look at Brian Spencer, who used to play for us. The crowd goes crazy with joy watching Spencer skate because he *looks* like he's working so damn hard, but he's not doing anything! There's no question that Clarke *does* a lot for the Flyers, and the other players see that and respond. Bobby skates with so much desire that it inevitably rubs off on his teammates.

A lot of the credit a man like Clarke brings to the Flyers is dissipated by some of the chintzy acts of his teammates. Bill Barber is one of the best forwards in the business, but he's also criticized because of his "swan-diving."

The way Barber executes his dives would make Rudolf Nureyev proud. If he's breaking through the enemy defenses and an opponent intercepts him with a slight hook or a legal hip check, Barber will suddenly go into orbit, rendering himself horizontal with such consummate skill that the referee believes Barber has been fouled and blows his whistle for a penalty against the innocent opponent. Once the whistle is blown, there's no calling back a player from the penalty box—though I'm sure that many a referee wished he could do just that after realizing he had been duped by the Bill Barber "swan dive."

I don't suggest that my teammates are entirely innocent of this maneuver. "Denis," Bert Marshall once suggested, "when you go for that puck, there are a lot of guys who hook you and hold you and get away with it without the ref calling the penalty he should. And the reason he doesn't call the penalty is that you keep on going. If you fell, he'd call a penalty." I understood Bert's point, but I told him I'd find it embarrassing to pull off a stunt like that the way Barber does. I'm strong on my skates, strong enough to shake them off.

"Look, Bert," I told Marshall, "I know there are lots of times when they'd call a penalty if I were to fall. But, hell, I've got the puck. And when I've got the puck, there's no way that I'm going to give it up by taking a dive, because there's just that chance that I *might* break through their defenses and get a shot on goal. To me that's the way to play hockey."

The way to play hockey against the Flyers is to treat them the way you handle the schoolyard bully: You have to give them back everything that they punish you with, and then some. There is no "secret" about the Flyers' success. Quite the contrary, their coach has always made a point about being completely open about his objectives and how he wants his players to fulfill them. He posts messages on the club bulletin board and then lets the reporters in to read them. On the eve of our opening game at Philadelphia's Spectrum, Shero had written the following message on the board:

"People can be divided into three parts. Those who make things happen. Those who watch things happen. And those who wonder what happened. In which category are you?"

If he had been asking us, and had the opening game of the semifinals in mind, the answer would have been the second category—we watched things happen. We watched the Flyers' goalie Bernie Parent get hurt in a pre-game warm-up and be replaced by second-stringer Wayne Stephenson and, instead of seizing their jugular, we watched the Flyers shoot four pucks past Glenn Resch. We got nothing! We made the fatal mistake of coming out on the ice and waiting to see what *they* were going to do. That was wrong, totally wrong. We should have gone right at them from the opening face-off, hitting them, skating hard, being aggressive. But we didn't do it. Instead, for some inexplicable reason, we laid back and waited to see what they'd do. We made the cardinal mistake of hockey—indecision.

Game two was even more frustrating, if that was possible. We were down, 4–1, tied the game, 4–4, and then lost in sudden-death overtime when Clarke kicked the puck into the net. It was an illegal goal, but the referee didn't call it. I don't blame Clarke; anyone would have done that. But I blame the guy who was running the game.

Blowing the thing after our comeback was really annoying. "It was," said Eddie Westfall, "like having two spares in the trunk and winding up with three flats."

For two games we had faced the Flyers' number two goalie, Wayne Stephenson. In game three, Freddie Shero, having learned that Bernie Parent's knee was better, decided to go with number one. Bernie shut us out, 1–0, not because he was sensational, but because we only threw 14 shots at him. So here we were, back where we had been with the Penguins, down three games and counted out by everyone—but ourselves.

What goes through an athlete's head when his team is backed up so hard against the wall there's nowhere to turn? The Islanders shared that experience twice in a period of a month, first with the Penguins and now with the Flyers. Confronted with elimination by Pittsburgh, I genuinely felt that nobody on the club had given up hope for survival. I felt precisely the same way when we found ourselves in the same situation against Philadelphia. But there was one significant difference: In the 1–0 loss to Philly, for example, we had played as good a defensive game as possible, but the offense hadn't done a thing. We couldn't muster the scoring power we needed to win. Could we do it in game four was the question now.

Our collective hearts actually stopped beating on Wednesday, May 7, 1975. It happened at precisely 20:00 of the third period. We had nursed a three-goal lead for 32 minutes when the roof fell in. One, two, three goals and the Flyers had tied it. Then, with the seconds ticking away in the third period and the score still tied, Reg Leach of the Flyers poked the puck past Resch just as the period-ending buzzer sounded. We were all in a state of shock. Our heads drooped in defeat and we prepared to line up for the traditional end-of-series handshaking ceremonies.

When referee Dave Newell rushed to the linesmen Claude Bechard and Leon Stickle, however, we realized that the game *wasn't* over. The goal was disallowed because it had entered the net a split second after the green light that signalled the end of the period had flashed. Given that new life, we were obligated to do something positive. At 1:55 of the sudden-death overtime, Jude Drouin won the game for us. The "miracle" headliners ran to their desks.

"The legend of the Islanders grew last night," wrote Bill Verigan of the *Daily News.*

A headline in *The Post* shouted: YES, THE ISLANDERS BELIEVE.

For the seventh time we had arrived at match-point, one swing away from Stanley Cup playoff elimination, and for the seventh time we literally fought back. We bombed the Flyers, 5–1, in their home rink and Dave Schultz was beaten to a pulp—*after* he had started a fight with our Clark Gillies—with a series of right-hand punches. Even *Philadelphia Bulletin* writer Jack Chevalier said it was Schultz's "worst beating of the season."

How could I explain this comeback after the last one? In Las Vegas the gamblers have an expression for a crapshooter who defies the laws of probability by making point after point on a hot roll: "He's unconscious," the stickmen say. Which is another way of saying that the lucky shooter is floating on such a high he doesn't realize what he's doing. Perhaps that was our secret. Perhaps if we had thought too deeply about our chances we would have realized we couldn't do it. But we never allowed negativism to intrude. Before game six I told a Montreal reporter who had phoned me that we'd beat the Flyers, 2–1, in the sixth game at Nassau Coliseum.

After 42 seconds of the first period I wished I had kept my big mouth shut. Ross Lonsberry, my candidate for most underrated player in the NHL, scored for the Flyers. As the red light went on, I remembered every game of the Pittsburgh series and every game of the Philly series. Until now, the team that scored first was the eventual winner.

Unfortunately, we were flat for too long at the start; hesitant, the way we were in the opening game of the series; thinking too much, not doing things naturally, as they come. We had to wake up. After the first period I could feel the tide turning, and I was the tide-maker. At 16:10 of the second period Bobby Clarke went into the penalty box and we cranked up our power play—the one the Rangers used to ridicule. On every power play you feel it's your big chance, and on this one Eddie Westfall got the puck to Jude Drouin. The pass Drouin gave me can only be described as ideal, and I had to make the split-second choice that happens over and over in a hockey game.

In taking my shot, should I crank up for the big "golf swing" and a slap shot or should I take a quick "wrist" shot with perhaps less velocity? I knew instinctively that if I wound up, Bernie Parent would have time to move one or two feet away from his cage, cutting off my shooting angle so that my shot would be likely to bounce harmlessly off his pads. I went for the flick of the wrist because it provided the element of surprise; the only way to catch a good goaltender is off guard, and that's precisely what I did. The shot wasn't that hard (standard misconceptions among naive hockey fans are that all shots have to be "hard" and that skaters should always skate "fast") but, more important, it was accurate and it skimmed across the ice low enough to elude Parent's vision.

All we had to do now was to put another one past Parent and hope that Resch would hermetically seal our net once more. My defensive sidekick, Gerry Hart, came through with the goal at 3:42 of the third period, and then Chico posted his "off-limits" sign. The series, incredibly, was tied at three apiece.

After the sixth game I sat down to get my thoughts together. The Islanders, in only their third year, were now one of just three teams left in the Stanley Cup homestretch.

If you think I was feeling spooky, imagine how the Flyers felt. Somebody told me that Philly defenseman Jim Watson said he thought the Flyers were playing against the devil. I know that if I had been in their skates, I'd have been damned worried. Some external force did seem to be going along with us, driving us, seeing us through, carrying the load. I began looking to see whether somebody up there really did like us.

Unfortunately, there was somebody who liked the Flyers more than us—Miss Kate Smith. The Flyers had to bring out the mighty Kate to sing *God Bless America,* the biggest good luck charm in professional sports. When Kate had sung that song in Philadelphia—live or on record—the Flyers had gone 40–3–1. We knew the Flyers would import Miss Smith, live, and we knew we had to out-psych them—somehow, some way.

We decided that just prior to Kate's singing of *God Bless America,* Eddie Westfall would present her with a bouquet of flowers from the Islanders and give her a kiss. And that would be the end of it. We didn't really worry about Kate's deciding the outcome of the game. But, inadvertently, she *did* hurt us. Here is how one game was turned around in the 15 minutes *before* the opening face-off.

Normally a pre-game ceremony prior to a Stanley Cup seventh game is short and sweet. That's because the game itself is all-important, and momentum is the pivotal factor. We were high as the sky when we left the dressing room for the opening face-off. Chico Resch, the backbone of our defense, was wound up beyond belief and ready to close the net once more. But, instead of being able to do our thing, we had to stand around like cigar store Indians while the endless Kate Smith ritual was performed. This consumed 15 minutes, time enough for Resch to cool from white hot to cold. "It isn't fair," said Chico. "Here we are, pumped up and ready to go, and we have to wait, and wait, and wait."

We knew Chico was cold before two minutes of the game had elapsed. Gary Dornhoefer lifted a long shot past Resch at 19 seconds, and a minute and eight seconds later Rick MacLeish made it 2–0. We never did recover; we skated off the ice at 10:45 P.M. empty of miracles. We were beaten 4–1 by a club that was better than we were in the game we had to win. But we never quit, and that earned us a lot of respect throughout the hockey world. I know because Freddie Shero echoed my feelings when he shook our hands and said:

"The Islanders have arrived."

# MY PERSONAL ALL-STARS

While the New York Islanders had "arrived" as a major factor in the NHL, the Philadelphia Flyers in May 1975 continued their own personal crusade to prove that they were not just one-time Stanley Cup champions. They made their point by defeating the Buffalo Sabres for their second straight indulgence in Cup champagne.

Despite their encore championship, the Flyers were still the subject of some skepticism among the hockey fraternity. But critics were guilty of a typical *faux pas* in evaluating talent: They looked for superstars instead of super players. The superstar is a skater who gets a lot of media coverage and, ultimately, appears to the press to be a better player than he appears to his opponents. The super player is one who may not obtain gallons of ink but who does the job—often subtly—on the ice and thereby gains the respect of his opponents. The Flyers were deserving champs because they had more super players than superstars.

Gary Dornhoefer never did and never will make a First All-Star Team, but he is first-rate in my book. He has the irrepressible knack of coming at you and at you and at you, often with his stick up. That can be awfully damaging to the palate, and I've developed a grand hate for Dornhoefer. What makes coping with him difficult is that there's nothing you can do about him after his initial charge. He's like The Shadow; a second later he seems to have disappeared.

One of Dornhoefer's most effective pastimes is planting his rather large frame in front of the goal crease so that he "screens" the goaltender from seeing the shot. As big as he is, Dornhoefer seems to appear in the goal area suddenly, before it's too late to move; next thing you know, the red light is on behind your goalie.

His colleague, Ross Lonsberry, is another unsung ace, one of the best wingers in the NHL. His moves are subtle and he drives defensemen crazy because he always seems to be right on top of you, forechecking like crazy. He hits you after you make a pass and he hits you after you take a shot. He keeps looking you right in the eye, keeps coming right at you.

Usually it takes a full season to get a book on some players. For the really good ones, those who don't always do the same things every time they have the puck, it can take even longer. Pit Martin stands out in my mind. He's a far better hockey player than he's given credit for, because he tries hard at all times. And he's very vicious, which is something that took me by surprise. If you bother him, he comes back at you, he retaliates in some way. That's the type of hockey player you can respect—and respect is very important in this game.

For natural talent, I would list a number of players. Orr, of course; Rick MacLeish, who does so much with his natural talent; Gil Perreault; Guy Lafleur; Jean Ratelle; Bryan Trottier; and maybe myself.

Guys like MacLeish are the ones you have to look out for. He's always behind you, always there, and he always has the puck. He's invariably either setting up a play for someone or getting ready to take a pass. Most important, he's never out of position. He not only has natural ability, he has its corollary, hockey sense, as well.

A player of that type, who disciplines his natural talent, is far more valuable a player than, say, Marcel Dionne of Los Angeles. When I heard that the Kings had traded for Dionne, I couldn't believe it. The Kings depend on tight, patterned checking, while Dionne is not a positional player at all. He's got great skating ability, a good shot, and good moves, but he just goes to the net.

My objections to Perreault and Lafleur are that they are uniquely offense-minded. When we played Buffalo in the 1976 Stanley Cup quarter-finals, we knew exactly where Perreault would stop in the offensive zone. Knowing that, it was simple to move him out. Lafleur didn't bother us much in the playoffs either, because we knew his moves as well. Guys like MacLeish, Ratelle, and Orr are totally unpredictable— and therefore far more difficult to stop.

The hardest hitter in the league by far is Dan Maloney of the Detroit Red Wings. Other good hitters are Dennis Owchar of the Penguins and Hilliard Graves of the Flames. These players step into you, which is very important. They are also good at moving right at you and cutting off your passing lanes. Some of them, such as Graves and Gary Dornhoefer of Philadelphia, keep coming at you after you've passed the puck, cutting off your skating lane, and leaving you little or no room to follow the play.

There are some players in the NHL who have undeserved reputations for hitting. The really good ones have the timing that allows them to get their entire bodies behind a check. Others, such as Ed Van Impe, now of Pittsburgh, need their sticks to guide you into the boards, where they hold you while they unload their check.

Larry Robinson of Montreal is a fairly good hitter, but he can't time his hits well enough to go after you. He's so big that, rather than go after you, he waits for you to crash into him. To get by him, you have to crash into him, because he's so strong. Pierre Bouchard of the Canadiens is the same type. They would rather meet you than go after you.

I'm something of a hitter myself. When I first came up, I told Al that if I were put on the left side, I'd be able to hit a lot more guys because I can run my left hip and leg into an attacker better than I can my right. But Al told me that, because I'm a lefthanded shot, my stick would be against the boards on the left side and my passing lanes would be cut off. It was true. That's why both Orr and Park play on the right side; it opens up the whole rink for passing and stickhandling. But I can still give forwards a good run.

One aspect of the game that has lost its stars is that of playmaking. When I think of playmakers, I remember Jean Beliveau and Doug Harvey. None of the guys today who have reputations as playmakers belong in that category—except perhaps Stan Mikita and Ratelle.

Bobby Orr is *not* a great playmaker in my book. He finishes a play for his club. He skates with the puck, gets around defenses, and creates offense, but he doesn't send guys in alone or draw three men in on him and make a good pass. That's what I expect from a playmaker.

Bobby Clarke is a hard worker. He rattles the other team's defense and causes mistakes with his persistence, and then Leach and Barber pick up the garbage. That, in a sense, is playmaking, but it's not moving a puck like the Beliveaus and the Harveys did.

Mikita and Ratelle are the best. Both handle the puck until they're double-teamed, then unload it to a winger who can go in free.

Pete Mahovlich is by no stretch of the imagination a playmaker. He never gives up the puck. He has to be ten feet inside the blue line, then see an opening that will allow him to go right in on net. If you check him, you nullify his wingers. That is why Lafleur played on the Jacques Lemaire line.

On the other hand, there are plenty of good shots these days. Rick Martin, Dennis Hull, Bobby Orr, Jacques Lemaire, Danny Grant, and Bill Goldsworthy all have great shots, both hard and accurate. I have a fairly accurate shot, and I can get rid of the puck quickly, but I don't have the respected shot that these shooters have.

Fast skaters are something the Islanders don't have. Billy Harris is a good skater, but he's not all that fast. Murray Wilson can beat anybody going from end to end. But Yvan Cournoyer has the fastest acceleration from the blue line to the net, which is most important when you're looking for speed. Some players, such as Steve Shutt of Montreal or Rick MacLeish, Reggie Leach, and Bill Barber of Philadelphia, position themselves so perfectly that they can receive a pass in full stride. It gives them an illusion of breakneck speed. If I had my choice for the Islanders, I'd want one of them.

The smartest players in the league right now, for my money, are those who always do the unexpected. Reggie Leach is smart because he knows what he can do, unlike a Perreault or a Lafleur. He shoots whenever he sees the daylight. Clarke is also very smart because he has an uncanny ability to rattle defensemen.

Both Park and Jean Ratelle are also continually doing the unexpected. (For that reason, I really like Ratelle.) MacLeish and Lonsberry of Philadelphia are also smart, as are Pierre Larouche and Jean Pronovost of Pittsburgh.

Goaltending has probably progressed more than any other aspect of the game. For natural talent, I think Dan Bouchard of Atlanta is the best of today's goaltenders because he has no weaknesses. He's strong on his stick and his glove side; he's good high and low. Most goaltenders give you some daylight to shoot at, then stop it. Bouchard doesn't give you anything. He's also the best goaltender in a scramble that I've ever seen. He can control the puck.

Parent is very good, as is Dryden. Both have an easier job because their clubs are so defense-minded. But Dryden, for example, is not as steady as Bouchard. Like all the Montreal goalies of the past few years, he goes down when there's a scramble in front of the net. In doing this, his sheer size allows no daylight down low. Up high, however, his mobility is restricted, and he can be beaten.But, like Bunny Larocque, he's trained that way. It's the percentage move, especially when there's a scramble in front.

Most goalies in the NHL would have to face five to ten more shots a game if it weren't for their defensive defensemen. I consider myself very good defensively, but there are guys out there solely for the purpose of blocking shots and playing defense. Borje Salming of the Maple Leafs is one of them. Salming plays the European style of game and, as a result, he often gets burned. Watching the 1976 Stanley Cup series between Toronto and Philadelphia on television, I noticed something different about Salming's game. He didn't take the guy out of the play but, instead, went down on one knee and swung his stick back and forth like a pendulum. Frequently it works for him. But he gets burned when the puck-carrier fakes his shot, goes right around him, and finds a clear path to the net.

There are several good defensive defensemen in the NHL, but the best one, all around, is Dave Burrows of the Pittsburgh Penguins. He's very much underrated. And the only people who are aware of it are the fans and the media in Pittsburgh—and the NHL forwards who can't get around him with the puck.

Jim Watson is very good, too, but I always had a great deal of respect for Bill White of Chicago as a good defensive defenseman. Lately, though, I think he's lost a step. He's not as strong as he used to be and it's reflected in his play, even if he still moves the puck very well.

Bobby Orr's style is strictly offensive, and the players in the NHL are aware of it. When I played against Boston and I carried the puck, I went right to Orr because I knew he was going to give me the blue line every time; and he never disappointed me. I couldn't go around him because he's still too good a skater. When I'd get a step on him, he would catch up instantly. I also knew that he wasn't going to hit me. Therefore I'd get the blue line on his side, look around for my teammates, and wait for them to make their moves to the net.

When a guy is skating on Orr, there's usually another guy backchecking who will pick him up. As far as I'm concerned, that is not the way for a defensive defenseman to protect his zone at all. If he's just spending his time looking for the loose puck he can pick up and move out with, then he's not working to create the play that will separate the puck and the opposing forward.

If the 1976 Stanley Cup playoffs proved anything, it was the value of the defensive forward. Until April 1976, Bob Gainey of the Canadiens was virtually unknown to the media—and, therefore, to the hockey world at large. But Gainey so effectively guarded our Billy Harris and then several of the Flyers' big guns that he became a byword overnight. Gainey, Don Luce of Buffalo, and the Islanders' Lorne Henning are among the most underrated players in the NHL. Henning is an example of a dedicated foot soldier whose value is recognized within our dressing room but not much beyond that. Lorne, who has developed into a superb penalty-killer, moves the puck well, plays a heady game, and has enormous stamina.

Critics of hockey often argue that unlike football, which relies on play after intricate play and hundreds of diagrams, hockey is merely "shinny," a game that relies more on brawn than brain.

This is hardly the case; our club pores over the play board almost every day of the season. We have meeting upon meeting to discuss strategies and hone various plays to sharpness. Some teams will work on a single play for years until it finally bears fruit. The Islanders were victimized by just such a play in our opening game with the Montreal Candiens in the Stanley Cup semi-finals in May 1976.

The score was 2–2 at the time, with the face-off deep in the New York zone to the right of the net. Only six minutes remained in the third period. To score the goal that beat us, 3–2, the Canadiens executed a play that had been formulated and modified *before the Islanders was even born!*

In 1970 Yvan Cournoyer and Jean Beliveau devised the play with Beliveau acting as center taking the face-off and Cournoyer as the wingman who would capture the puck from the draw. (Beliveau revealed the secret of the play and its roots after Cournoyer had successfully used it—with Jacques Lemaire replacing the retired Beliveau—against us.)

"When I centered for Yvan," Beliveau explained, "the idea was for me to win the face-off and pass the puck back to a designated spot about ten feet to my left and about ten feet left of where Cournoyer was standing, prior to the dropping of the puck.

"Surprise is essential to its success; in other words, the play cannot be used consistently. We would try it every once in a while and soon realized that it occasionally worked, and when it worked, of course, we scored a goal."

The Canadiens refined and refined the process and, when Beliveau retired, Lemaire took up where Jean had left off and the Cournoyer-Lemaire combination worked it to perfection in a mere three seconds and thereby turned the series in Montreal's favor. Here's what happened:

1. Lemaire won the face-off and skimmed the puck backhanded to the predetermined "meeting" point for Cournoyer.

2. Cournoyer raced from his check just *before* the puck was

dropped by the linesman, keeping outside the circle as the rules require. As a result, Cournoyer had a full head of steam on reaching the meeting point with the puck.

3. As Lemaire moved the puck from the face-off circle to Cournoyer, their linemate, Yvan Lambert, sped toward our net in order to screen our goaltender.

4. Although we reacted to all the Canadiens' moves, Cournoyer had enough of a jump on us to move into position for a shot at the unscreened portion of the net. Needless to say, he found the mark.

The key to this play was surprise. Until that point in the game Cournoyer had always rushed forward, seemingly to pick up any loose puck on the right side or in the corner. This time Yvan The Terrible crossed up and went left—and there went the game for us!

After we had been knocked out of the 1976 semi-finals in five games, Montreal's coach Scotty Bowman revealed that the Canadiens employ 12 such "specialty plays" which are constantly practiced and used only on precise occasions when they might fit into a goal-getting— or game-winning—situation.

So much for those who argue that hockey is not a thinking-man's game.

My personal All-Star list includes still another important category: players with whom I can relate intellectually. It may sound presumptuous, but I like to think that there is more to life than the hockey rink, and I naturally gravitate to players who think like me. In that sense, my defense partner, Gerry Hart, ranks high on my personal All-Star Team.

To those who don't know Gerry, he comes off as a rugged, often pugnacious guy whose only interests are blocking pucks and hitting bodies. But Hart is actually a rather sophisticated guy who is a master cook, an excellent boatman, and, like myself, a perfectionist in almost everything he tries. He can discuss his favorite subjects with more than just a minute or two of superficial gab, and he *is* opinionated—which I like because I am, too.

I want to be able to talk about *any* subject, and to be able to do that, I know I have to read every book that I can lay my hands on and that I can find time to read. I've found that I can talk about a lot of things with the older guys like Eddie Westfall and J. P. Parise because they have opinions on everything, not just hockey. This is very important to me.

# 16

# DENIS POTVIN'S *PEOPLE &* OTHER *PROPERTIES*

Before I was old enough to vote—or to play professional hockey—I sensed that there was something significantly different about my outlook toward life compared with that of my contemporaries on the Ottawa 67s. Their goals had a common denominator: to play hockey for the sake of playing hockey, period. Their world extended from one end of the rink to the other and culminated in the dressing room. The outside world existed only to the extent that it enabled them to commute from one hockey rink to another.

Like my contemporaries, I loved hockey then more than anything else in life. But hockey was more than the physical sensation of body crunching against body, the orgasmic delight of seeing the black hunk of vulcanized rubber penetrate the deepest recesses of the net, and the camaraderie of the team. Hockey had a very definite *purpose* to me. It was fulfilling my objectives of worldliness, security, and the need to do what my father never could—pick and choose.

To me hockey is a great joy and an immense ego-inflator, but more than anything it is a business. If I had any doubts about this at age 17, they were thoroughly dispelled by age 19, when I still was an amateur and living with my mother and father in Ottawa. It was then that Ray Volpe from NHL Services, Inc., first phoned from Manhattan and asked me to come to New York to do a commercial for Pepsi-Cola. When they made reservations for me at the Plaza Hotel, I understood that hockey would be the ideal vehicle for opening doors in business, that fascinating continent I wanted very much to explore.

Among my first impressions after I had come to live in the New York area was that there was a distinct difference between the "American" and the "Canadian." Generalizations can be all wet, but I felt that Americans, as a rule, were considerably more confident, more dynamic, and more positive than my Canadian compatriots.

Perhaps it is a function of America's independence—Canada, after all, has been tied to Great Britain all its life, and still is—as well as the country's vast growth and power. In Canada, few gambles are taken in politics or in everyday life, the people tend to be more conservative, and a Canadian is more content to remain at the same level of mediocrity for the rest of his life.

But I could see that Americans pay the price for this distinction. The pace in New York is so much faster and the people appear to be under greater strain. It suddenly came to me one day: At last, I realized, I am witnessing the "rat race." And it's not all that bad!

Meeting Volpe, and later his colleagues at the NHL, Tony Andrea and Edd Griles, was a pivotal move for me, although I didn't know it then. By the time the Flyers had eliminated us from the playoffs in 1975 my outlook had broadened considerably. I was convinced that, even though I had already made a name in hockey, I wanted to waste no time making my name in marketing. This was a field that had always intrigued me and one that I could enter at age 22, thanks to my connections with Andrea and Griles, who left the NHL in the summer of 1975 to form an outfit called People & Properties.

When they expressed an interest in me, I leaped at the chance to become involved with them because, again, it set me apart from the traditional hockey player in an exceptionally relevant way. I was already doing something that was not only rare for a player at this stage in his career but something many players don't do even when they are 32— that is, seeking an alternative to hockey. The average puck-pusher doesn't even *start* thinking about an alternate vocation until he's in his late twenties or early thirties. Then, all of a sudden, he'll be scrambling around, looking for something, anything, to do when his playing career is finished.

I made a deal with Andrea to learn the marketing business in the summertime so that when I reached 30 and was ready to retire from the NHL I'd be able to step right in and give the company as much as it's going to give me. I don't want to be just another jock who lends his name and nothing else to a firm; I want to be able to learn the business, do the work, and be good at it. I want very much to go out and meet all kinds of people—not just hockey people—and I want to have my own office, sit behind a desk, and be a big businessman in my own right.

Behind all this was my motivating factor from the time I made my commitment to professional hockey: security. Remember, my father thought he would be a pro with the Detroit Red Wings—but one false move at a training camp and he never saw the light of day in the NHL. I had to have a stepping-stone to other realms in the event hockey couldn't support me.

When I became a part of People & Properties, I made a critical decision: I changed agents and entered into one of the most unusual contract negotiations the sports world has known.

As the 1974–75 season came to an end, I was in the midst of a falling out with my Montreal representatives, Dave Schatia and Larry Sazant. One problem piled on another until, finally, I went to Ray Volpe and asked if he had any ideas about someone else who could represent me.

I had expected to hear a name as familiar as those of Al Eagleson, Fred Sharf, Larry Rauch, and Schatia and Sazant, but he mentioned David Cogan.

"Who is he?" I asked.

"He's a top negotiator in the entertainment business," said Tony Andrea. "A very, very tough man. Go see him and let me know what you think."

Cogan's office is located near the top of the Empire State Building and has a panoramic view of the East Side of Manhattan and the borough of Queens. We sat on his couch and talked turkey. I was impressed. Unlike the others, Cogan told me that I didn't have to sign anything and I could leave him anytime I wanted. What a sense of freedom. And I understood everything he said.

I told one of the Islanders about Cogan, and he said, "but he never handled a hockey player."

I figured that a guy who did nothing but handle hockey players couldn't be good for me. I learned from my teammates that some of the guys who only handle hockey players were said to make under-the-table deals with the club general manager and the team. I did have an arrangement with Schatia and Sazant; they were ready to negotiate a new contract for me in 1975.

My parting with Schatia and Sazant was accompanied by mixed emotions. On the one hand we had differences over how certain matters should be handled but nevertheless I did feel a certain warmth for them. After all they were my first agents and I did appreciate a lot of things they had done for me. I'll never forget them for that.

On the other hand, I had to chart the course that I believed was the best for me and my family. With that in mind, I decided to have Cogan as my representative. The new contract game in 1975–76 now featured

David Cogan and Denis Potvin on one side and Bill Torrey and Roy Boe, the Islanders' owner, on the other.

Cogan was on the phone with me every single day, starting in late August 1975 when he opened his talks with Torrey. Lots of times he'd call and throw questions at me just to see how I would react and how much interest I had. When he saw how involved I was, he seemed pleased. By September, David Cogan and Denis Potvin had achieved total communication.

The biggest obstacle in the negotiations was basic salary. The Islanders' people wouldn't go for our demands for bonus clauses on the ground that the Islanders would be paying me lots of money to start with, enough incentive that I should be able to reach those goals. "It's ridiculous to give you a bonus after scoring ten or even 25 goals," said Torrey. And I had to agree with that thinking.

After several weeks of intensive negotiations, I began to see progress. One factor in my favor was that not only Cogan but Torrey, too, seemed to be in my corner. Whenever we'd reach a critical point, Bill would call and explain what had been worked out. "Are you happy with it?" was his standard question. I sensed that he was being honest with me and I felt quite good as the negotiations progressed.

I knew we were in good shape when Roy Boe and Torrey went to the Empire State Building and met Cogan for lunch. To me it appeared as if everyone were trying to *help* me, as if I were coping with a real dilemma and these people were trying to help me resolve it. Well, they certainly did. The final contract was a five-year deal with payment to be spread over a period of eight years. In other words, if after five years I retire, play for another team, or sign another contract, I will still receive my same salary for three more years—money I will have earned during the five years of my contract. The Islanders felt that they could live with the deal since it enabled them to spread out my salary payments over a longer period.

But it wasn't until February 1976 that we began to see light at the end of the contract tunnel. The central concern was putting a price on my value to the team. To do that, I had to determine—with a little help from Cogan—precisely what my value was to the team and to the NHL. I put the question to myself: Denis, how do you assess your value? My answer lay in the ascent of the Islanders since I arrived in Uniondale in 1973.

Obviously I couldn't take all the credit for the improvement, but there was tangible evidence that I had done much to bring the Islanders to the point where they were selling out practically every game. The gate has gone up about 30 percent since I first put on the Islanders' jersey.

There were other aspects of my value. The fact that I was immediately visible and highly publicized even before I came to the NHL reflected on the Islanders. Our goals-against record kept going down. I don't for a minute overlook the contributions of Bert Marshall, Gerry Hart, Dave Lewis, Brother Jean, or Dave Fortier, but it was clear that what the club's defense had needed was a "flexible anchor," a guy who could do it all—play back and kill penalties when necessary, work the power play, take a regular shift, and lead. I knew I could play up to 45 of the 60 minutes in a game, and I knew I wasn't going to miss more than a handful of games each season. All these factors were valuable and they all added up in determining my worth.

I compared myself with some other "name" defensemen around the league, guys like Jim Schoenfeld, captain of the Buffalo Sabres. No doubt Schoenfeld is tremendously valuable to Buffalo, and I'm sure he's well paid. But here's a guy who misses 20 games a year. Schoenfeld has been playing for four years and every year he's been out something like two dozen or more games. It's the same thing with Brad Park. If it isn't his knee, it's something else. And I don't have to go into the Bobby Orr situation. His reliability is uncertain even from period to period.

I've had tremendous staying power right from the start, and that's been a big plus for me. I can play with a broken foot when other guys would take themselves out of a game. I can play with a charley horse while others won't. Other guys don't work as hard to return from an injury as I do. I have a very firm policy: *I don't want to miss a game if I can help it.* I missed one game my first year, one game my second year and two games in 1975–76. That's not bad, considering the amount of time I put in.

Finally, there was the image I was helping to create for the team—a positive image. While the media remained highly critical of the Rangers' players and their lack of communication, the reporters time and again commended me for my patience and articulation. I represented the Islanders well off the ice, and I encouraged my teammates to do the same.

Bryan Trottier, for example, was only 19 in his rookie season (1975–76) and extremely bashful and hesitant about dealing with the press. I talked with him about it whenever I could. "Don't let them bother you," was my advice. "Just talk, but don't incriminate yourself. If you must incriminate yourself, do it for a feature story, don't do it for the next day's paper." The team assigned Trottier the dressing cubicle next to mine and he watched the ease with which I dealt with the media. Pretty soon it rubbed off on him.

I added up all these plusses and came to the conclusion that I was worth a fair amount of money to the team. Now the question was whether the Islanders—particularly Roy Boe and Bill Torrey—shared my evaluation of Denis Potvin. A lot hinged on my play during the early part of the 1975–76 season when the negotiations were building toward a climax. A couple of big boo-boos and I might really have screwed things up.

Instead of passing the mess out of my mind, I'd carry it into a game, worrying like hell about what was going to happen. My game went from modest to mediocre; the more I thought about the problem, the more my game deteriorated. I stopped being the aggressor and began to let the enemy dictate the play to me. Finally, I had a personal showdown with myself.

Denis, I said, for the sake of the team and the sake of your own well-being, you've got to stop worrying and start playing hockey like you can. Get mad. If you have aggressions, take them out on the other team. Use your anger to your own advantage.

One episode more than any other triggered this anger and turned it in the right direction. We were in Pittsburgh, losing, 2–1, at the end of the first period. I was in the middle of my "downer" over the Schatia-Sazant business, and during that opening 20 minutes I had just been dragging my ass around the rink.

Up to this point in the season, Al Arbour had been very patient and very tolerant with me. Al knew by now that nothing bugs me more than being embarrassed in front of my own teammates. I knew that if Al gave me grief about anything, he had a damn good reason for doing so. That night at Pittsburgh he *did* have reason.

He walked into the room after the period was over, pulled on his glasses, and turned in my direction. "Denis," he said. "Sonofabitch, it's one thing to look like you're carrying a piano on your back during the game, *but it's another thing to stop and play it!*"

It might have been Al's funniest line ever, but at that moment I couldn't applaud the humor. My face just dropped; I got hot and red and I just sat there, as pissed off as I had ever been in my life. The entire room was silent.

I had been holding an orange in my hand when Al walked in. When the coach finished what he had to say, I stood, cocked my arm, and hurled it against the wall. I watched it smash and saw the juice ooze slowly down the wall. It was excellent catharsis. A few minutes later we trooped out on the ice. I got started, the team got started, and we wound up whipping the Penguins' asses.

We put all the pieces of the contract together in mid-January, and it was a truly emotional moment for me when I realized that we had finally reached complete agreement. My first contract, big as it had been, was not something I felt I had *earned* at the time of the signing in 1973. It was as if the Islanders were paying a lot of money to me when I had not yet proven that I was worth a cent of it—sort of like buying an expensive car but not being sure it would do the job until you had it on the road for a while. But now I *had* been on the ice, and for more than a while. My team had made the playoffs, I was an All-Star, and my heart tingled in an upbeat way.

The 1976 agreement was The Contract. It was so big and it was so good that I felt a need to have my parents on hand in David Cogan's office when I signed it. This was at the time that we were due to play the Soviet Wings team at Nassau Coliseum, and I had already invited my parents to New York to see the game.

Cogan was touched when I let him know I wanted my folks to be present when Debbie and I came for the signing. Up to then I had thought him a cold, hard-nosed businessman with little sensitivity for the down-home stuff like impressing your parents with a job well done. And I wondered how Armand Potvin, the white-collar French-Canadian, would react to David Cogan, the intense, big-time New York City negotiator.

The opening scene wasn't encouraging. My folks came to the Empire State Building and Cogan's impressive office, with Xerox machines, computers, and the usual trappings of upbeat Manhattan. In David's office there were the usual amenities.

The conversation got sticky and I began squirming, hoping someone would break the ice and ease the tension. Cogan gave my parents a tour of the office. "We've got 40 people working here," David said.

Armand Potvin wasn't impressed.

"Have you ever represented a hockey player before?" he shot back.

"No. Denis is the first hockey player I've ever handled. And, I'll tell you, Mr. Potvin, it's been a great challenge."

Then Mom cut in: "Can you *really* take care of my Denis?"

Cogan, who has a way of wrinkling his brows so that it appears that he has four deep canals running from ear to ear, turned from a frown to a smile. "Unfortunately, Mrs. Potvin, Denis can't have his parents here in New York, so, if you don't mind, I take your place!"

With that, my parents fell in love with David Cogan.

But my parents never miss a trick, so a few minutes later, when Dad took me aside to tell me he was impressed, I knew that *everything* about the contract signing was A-1. Their intuition is impeccably good.

And so, by the way, was the contract.

# 17

# I'M NAKED—AND THERE ARE TWO WOMEN IN THE DRESSING ROOM

The fact that we signed the new contract near the top of the Empire State Building meant more than that I was number one in New York hockey. It underlined my feeling that, unlike the average hockey player, I am a cosmopolitan man. They're afraid of New York; I love it. They turn away from it, but Debbie and I have studied it, travelled it from top to bottom, learned about it, and learned to love it.

I love walking in the city, from the Bowery to Washington Heights. I feel a part of it in almost every conceivable way, from its night life to its newspapers. It was tough for me at first; I tried to do everything and there was too much. Then I learned to be selective, to do those things that most interested me, and I learned more that way.

Debbie and I hunt out antiques at auction sales on Long Island and Connecticut. We picked up a big breakfront, for example, a beautiful 19th-century piece, for $900, about a third of what it's worth. Debbie is sharper than I am, but we're still not at the point where we can purchase a painting as an investment and be sure it will appreciate in value. At best, we can probably make more educated guesses than we could a few years ago. And we're more apt to pay $400 than $4,000 for a painting, but we do want art in our home. Once we went to a showing of Matisse and other greats. We planned to stop in for a few minutes and stayed for hours. It was one of the most thrilling days I've spent.

Our experiences in New York have taught us a lot, but exciting as it has been, it seems hardly anything so far. I happen to think that what I've done isn't bad for a guy of 23 with no more than a high school education—but then that is a prejudiced opinion, and besides, I have probably been unusually fortunate in my directions.

Most of my teammates, on the other hand, have all these same nonsporting riches available just for the asking, and yet are so sadly ignorant of many of them.

I guess you'd have to say many of them just kill time between games. Many are growing, but many are not. Many are wasting their youth. Many are wasting New York City. You read about the problems of life in New York City and you forget that the city has more to offer than any other in this part of the world. It seems a shame that many don't take advantage of it. Most don't even do the tourist things.

The problem, of course, is that most hockey players come from small Canadian towns and, like all kids, are impressionable. Their first ideas about New York inevitably are negative and, I'm sure, they retain these ideas when they come to the city. It might not even be so bad if we had more time to see other cities on the road, but travel is so tight these days you don't get to see much more than the airport, the airplane, the bus, the hotel and the arena.

So Debbie and I plan to see as much of other cities and other countries as we can during the off-season. Even if few people our age, outside of sports of course, make the kind of money to do these things—we have been most fortunate to have been all but adopted by many of our older neighbors. They encourage us to expand our horizons, and for me, to prepare for the inevitable day when I can no longer play.

I love hockey and I hope to play a long time, but you're usually finished before you're even 40! I want to be ready for a life beyond the rink. I don't want to waste my youth, and even though I've only begun in hockey, I've already begun my own business. But I'm fully aware that none of these good things would have been possible had I not been fortunate enough to find a wife who was patient, who could share them with me and grow with me as a person as I believe I have grown.

It's not easy being the wife of a hockey player. This was a point I constantly emphasized with Debbie before we were married. We'd take long walks and have long discussions about what it would be like for her to be my wife. It's like being the wife of a truck driver or a travelling salesman in the sense that, for a good part of the year, from training camp in October until the end of the playoffs in spring, I would rarely be home. Then there's the problem of having a husband who's a public figure who will have to spend a good part of his time trying to elude squealing fans, many of them female. "You will have to be strong, patient, and love me very much," I told her.

As much as I was in love with Debbie, I tried very hard to be a realist about the marital situation. I know that jealousy is a factor in everyone's psyche and that it doesn't have to be limited to the jealousy of one individual; she could wind up being jealous of the team, or jealous of my life style, or even jealous of something material of which I might be completely unaware at the time. I had to stress to Debbie that hockey was not going to slip conveniently away, that it is material, it's strong, it's with us, and it will involve hundreds of people with whom she, too, would become involved.

Debbie accepted this with as much foresight as possible and, as far as I'm concerned, her adjustment to the life of a "hockey wife" has been splendid. Every so often we'll talk about this and I'll learn that she sometimes suffers a not unexpected sadness about it all.

"We seem to be saying all the time, 'Oh, you didn't tell me that,' " Debbie once remarked. "We spend so much time apart we can't always catch up. We can't seem to get together and lead one life."

I had assumed that one of the biggest drawbacks for her was that I would be away for such long stretches of time. But Debbie accepted that and even found some good in the adversity. "Travel enhances the marriage to a certain extent," she explained. "The last few hours before you come home from a trip are exciting. It's the anticipation. I take a bath, fix up my hair, and hope that you're doing the same thing. But, as they say, a little water on the fire sparks it and too much extinguishes it."

By far the most grating damage to her ego is the constant attention I receive and the endless work I'm able to put into my profession while Debbie, an intelligent woman, does not yet have the chance to fulfill her intellectual potential.

One day she told me straight out: "All of a sudden I feel lost. I'm not doing a lot. My only outlet is you. I don't have the personal recognition and, at times, I find that my mind is shrinking rather than growing. I know it happens to other hockey wives, but I don't think they're as aware of it as I am."

As Debbie and other hockey wives have learned (many to their great consternation), they are *not* the only women in hockey. There are women in the front office; there are women who now teach "power skating" to professional hockey players, and there are women on the journalistic hockey beat.

"My God!" shouted Terry O'Reilly of the Boston Bruins. "This is something else!" And with that, a thoroughly undraped O'Reilly ran like hell into the dressing room shower at The Forum in Montreal.

A split second later, Bobby Orr threw on a towel and darted into the shower room after O'Reilly, who by this time had covered himself up. Phil Esposito, who was standing in the corner of the room, shook his head and moaned, "Maybe I'm old-fashioned, but this is going a little too far."

It was 10:30 P.M. in the dressing room of the Clarence Campbell Conference All-Star Team, Tuesday, January 21, 1975. For the first time in NHL history women reporters had invaded the players' dressing room along with their male counterparts, immediately after the game, while the athletes were undressing for their post-game shower. In the next few minutes, tough, hard-nosed players would display chaos and panic unlike anything they might betray in a Stanley Cup final.

The man who permitted the furor to develop in the first place was Armand "Bep" Guidolin, one of the two All-Star Game coaches. "They can go in," Guidolin said, "because I'm the coach and I think it's the right thing to do."

Guidolin wasn't without precedent. Women have been associated with hockey ever since the invention of the rubber puck. One of the NHL's most revered prizes is the Lady Byng Memorial Trophy, an annual award "to the player adjudged to have exhibited the best type of sportsmanship and gentlemanly conduct combined with a high standard of playing ability."

The trophy was originally presented to the NHL in 1925 by Lady Byng, wife of Canada's Governor-General at the time, and has been part of the woof and warp of hockey ever since. Long before the 1975 All-Star Game episode there were women on the hockey beat, if not in the dressing room mingling with naked players. Margaret Scott wrote about the Toronto Maple Leafs for years in the forties and fifties for *The Hockey News* and other publications. The first woman to author a full-length hockey book was Shirley Walton Fischler, who wrote *Up From the Minor Leagues of Hockey* and later co-authored a hockey encyclopedia.

It was Shirley, more than any other, who paved the way for the equal opportunity women later enjoyed on the hockey beat. She became co-editor in 1971 of *Action Sports Hockey,* a monthly publication, and began writing her own hockey column, "Shirley On Shinny." The content of the column was so powerful in its ideas, influence and language that it angered the Establishment and Shirley was barred from sitting in the Madison Square Garden press box alongside male hockey writers. She took the case to the New York City Human Rights Commission and brought the Garden to its knees. They agreed that women and men could sit side by side in the press box and, with that other women began covering hockey following Shirley's landmark triumph.

But none of the female hockey writers had ever tried to get into the dressing room immediately after the game. When Shirley was on a post-game story, she either entered the coach's room and asked her questions there or waited until the players were fully dressed and *out* of the dressing room before talking with them.

Everything changed on the night of January 21, 1975, at Montreal's Forum.

The game had ended a few minutes earlier and, as usual, the reporters—all male—began trooping into the dressing room, huddling around the more articulate skaters, pumping them with the usual questions. I spoke to a couple of them, then excused myself to take a shower. I still had a towel around my waist when I returned and began clearing away the skates and other equipment from my cubicle. Tracy Pratt, the whimsical Vancouver Canucks defenseman, was seated alongside me.

As I put my skates in order, I turned around—and standing directly in front of me was a woman dressed in a black outfit, holding a notebook in her left hand and a pen in her right. I gulped twice, trying to suppress the shock, and blurted, "What are *you* doing here?"

It was Robin Herman of *The New York Times,* who had been covering the Islanders all season. She didn't say a word. I looked across the room and gulped again. In a gray, two-piece dress with a blue blouse was an attractive woman wearing dark glasses and holding a microphone labelled "CKLM—1570" across the top. She was Marcelle Saint-Cyr, a reporter for a French-language station. Marcelle was confronting Guy Lafleur of the Canadiens.

Lafleur's entire backside was exposed, but he gingerly held a towel in front of his private parts while Marcelle conducted the interview.

Most of the other guys were standing against the walls by now, with towels wrapped around themselves and shit-assed grins on their faces. The moment Robin began asking me questions, Tracy Pratt reached over and, like a kid in a summer camp, pulled the towel off my body. I grabbed another and put it on, but Tracy hauled that one off just as fast. I was naked and there were two women in the dressing room. A first for Denis Potvin. But I was determined not to make a farce out of the situation; I just stared right into Robin's eyes, and she never lost my gaze. I'm sure she was more embarrassed than I was because she was in my territory and it was understood that I wouldn't have any clothes on.

Don Luce of Buffalo and some of the other guys stayed cool, making no attempt at modesty, and, naturally, there was the expected humor. "This," chirped Terry Harper of Los Angeles, "is better than the game."

Not long after the incident Robin presented me with a bottle of my favorite Scotch. "This," she said, "is a token of my appreciation for handling the situation fairly and without trying to embarrass me!"

The episode certainly generated as much publicity as the game. I picked up the French-language daily, *Montreal Matin,* and found this headline splashed across the sports page: DES DAMES AU VESTIAIRE (Women in the Dressing Room). The *Journal de Montreal* screamed: LES JOUEURS PLUS GÊNÉS QUE LES SCRIBES FÉMININS (The Players Were More Embarrassed Than the Women Writers).

Later I read the best headline of all in the *Chicago Daily News:* NHL "COVER-UP": WOMEN IN LOCKER ROOM!

Once the humor had subsided, the question was raised on every NHL team: Should women be permitted in the dressing room immediately after a game?

My answer is an unequivocal *no!* I believe that it's morally wrong and has bad effects on the married players with children. Debbie agrees with me. Think of the players' children. Think of the families. Imagine a nine-year-old asking, "Mommy, Mommy, why is that lady going into Daddy's dressing room?" That kid knows that we undress in the locker room and that there are separate men's rooms and ladies' rooms—and for a very good reason.

Apart from the moral issue, there's the matter of the players' feelings. When the women walked in, the entire atmosphere changed for the worse. We were uncomfortable; so were the other members of the media. One of the women mentioned that female reporters had been inside the pro basketball dressing rooms, but I wasn't impressed by that explanation. Basketball players have different temperaments than Canadian hockey players like myself. Needless to say, my opinion wasn't the only one solicited in this growing dispute.

The All-Star Game incident was the opening gun in a season-long battle over whether or not women should be permitted in our room. Finally Bill Torrey decided to put it to the players. We were in Kansas City for a game with the Scouts when Bill walked into the room about an hour before the opening face-off.

"Don't anybody get undressed," he shouted. "Robin Herman would like to come in and have a few words with you."

We all knew what this was about. She had already spoken to players individually and had gotten negative reactions. This time she must have figured we might react differently as a group with her there in the room.

"Look," she said, "I'm covering this team just as the male reporters are, and I have a deadline the same as they do. If I can't get into the room when they walk in, I can't get my stories in to my paper in time to beat the deadline. I want my information first-hand, not second-hand."

Robin asked us to take a vote and to let her know as soon as possible about changing the no-women-in-the-room regulation. We agreed to have a meeting and Eddie Westfall promised her an answer within a week.

We didn't have to wait a week; the minute Robin walked out the door we had the answer—an emphatic *no!* A couple of guys waffled on the issue, but not one Islander said he felt we definitely should let her in.

Al Arbour came up with an amusing "compromise" suggestion. He told us about a situation in pro football where the coach of a team had let a lady reporter in the dressing room—but only after the players had put blindfolds over *their* eyes.

Al wasn't suggesting we do that; he was reminding us that the dressing room belonged to the players. "You have the run of it," said Arbour. "Do what you want with it."

We stuck with our decision not to let women in the room. The Rangers made a similar decision after the Ranger wives became publicly vocal on the issue. However, we wanted to give Robin the same opportunity as her male competitors to meet her deadline. So we worked out a compromise: After a game, Robin goes to an area near the dressing room where our publicity man, Hawley Chester III, awaits her. She tells Hawley which players she'd like to interview. Hawley then goes into the dressing room and finds the players, and they come outside, in uniform, and talk with her.

We respect the job she has to do and we feel she is receiving equal, if separate, treatment.

# 18

# MORE THAN MEETS THE ICE

"Nail 'im, Denis! Nail 'im!"

The imploring shriek came from the Islanders' bench immediately to my right. I was backpedalling like a madman, my shoulders hunched forward, my eyes riveted on the enemy bearing down on me, my sharply honed skates churning the ice into snow as I moved backwards past my team's bench.

The guys were screaming instructions to me because the foe, in this case Floyd Thomson of the St. Louis Blues, made a desperate effort to outflank me by squeezing between me and the sideboards on my right and then swerving sharply to his right for a play on goal. Picking up my teammates' radar, I sensed instantly that I could make mincemeat out of Thomson's six feet, 190 pounds. He was like a jackrabbit speeding for the cover of a tree as the falcon dives to nail the prey. Too often the rabbit never makes it to the safety of the bush, and this time Thomson did not leap fast enough for the opening.

A swell of anger—perhaps the intensity elevates the sensation to raw, impersonal hatred—surged through me a split second before impact. It was as if all the sins of commission on defense could instantly be expiated in the simple mashing of Floyd Thomson by 205 pounds working like a human pile driver.

By sheer coincidence, my shoulders crunched into the St. Louis forward precisely at the moment he reached the far end of the Islanders' bench, where a pane of unbreakable protective glass abruptly intrudes above the wooden boards. As my body thumped Thomson, his head lurched back and collided full force with the lightly padded upright. A second after impact, I felt that I had synchronized my wallop so perfectly that Thomson had just blown away.

Next thing I hear is a whistle. I turned around and there was poor

Thomson stretched out on the ice looking very much like a victim of sudden death. My stomach nearly fell to my feet, I was so scared at what I had done to the guy. I apologize, Floyd, I said to myself, knowing I couldn't do it verbally just then.

I found that I was fighting an inner battle over what to do next. There was a consummate feeling of satisfaction over having delivered the perfect bodycheck—under the circumstances—and a terrible feeling of guilt over having pulverized someone I didn't even know. I worried that the enemy might close in on me, yet I knew that was a paranoid reaction; the referee hadn't called a penalty on the play so, it was obviously a legal check. Then one of the Blues came over to me. There was no hostility. "Do you think he's really hurt?" I asked, just to spark some conversation.

A second later I had my answer: His body began contorting with convulsions. "He's swallowing his tongue," somebody shouted. Our young trainer, Ron Waske, rushed over to Thomson, forced Thomson's mouth open, and got his forceps on Thomson's tongue to keep it from going down his throat. They wheeled out a stretcher and took Thomson to the hospital; he had suffered a concussion. I suffered a migraine and a day of guilt until I learned that my victim was out of danger. It had once again revealed the split feelings: I wanted to hurt him when I originally dealt the bodycheck, but I didn't want him hurt once I saw him writhing on the ice.

It has been said, and with justification, that a hockey player who thinks about—and therefore worries about—being injured in a game should not be playing. I subscribe to that theory and rarely, if ever, find myself worrying about wounds.

Although there have been deaths as a direct result of a game—the last one in the NHL occurred in 1968 when Bill Masterton of the Minnesota North Stars died following a severe bodycheck in a match with Oakland—there was one occasion in my own career when I actually suffered through a genuine and pervasive fear that I would die as a consequence of a game.

The mental brush with death developed on a Sunday night in my second NHL season, following a game at The Spectrum in Philadelphia. We had played an especially brutal game with the Boston Bruins on Saturday night at home, and on Sunday Al had me on the ice for at least 47 of the 60 minutes of playing time.

I loved it, just as I loved being on the ice so much of the game. I was sharp and, while I was on the ice, I didn't mind the oppressive heat in the arena. After the game I had a cold drink in the dressing room and later a beer on the team bus heading back to New York.

Suddenly, less than an hour out of Philly, I began experiencing shock waves of cramps, first in my arms and then in my legs. I got out of my seat and stood on my heels—anything to rid myself of this awful, growing pain.

But the cramps kept returning and I felt myself becoming dizzy. I imagined the beer was so cold and my body temperature still so warm that my body couldn't adjust to the point and counterpoint.

In a matter of a minute or two my hands and forehead were enveloped in perspiration and I was rapidly turning white. The guys didn't notice my torment at first, but soon it became apparent that I wasn't standing up because I liked to look out the front window of the bus.

One of the players asked what was bothering me.

I tried to answer but I had the terrible feeling that *I couldn't actually talk*.

"Hey," one of the voices piped up, "are you gonna swallow your tongue?"

Eddie Westfall had the bus driver pull over to a phone booth and they called an ambulance for me. We were at a town called Mount Holly, New Jersey, about 40 miles from Philadelphia, but I felt very close to hell at that moment.

The cramps up and down my body gave it the feeling of a series of giant pliers clamped at various parts of my body, pulling in different directions. Worst of all was the wrenching sensation in my chest.

It was then that I actually endured that miserable awareness that, maybe, it was all over; I thought my heart was going to stop beating. Denis, I cried to myself, you might be dead in another minute.

I had very little time to feel sorry for myself or to begin a lifetime of flashbacks. The ambulance arrived quickly and I was immediately laid on my back—whereupon I felt a tremendous relief. Coach Arbour accompanied me to the hospital, and that was a real morale booster.

After six glasses of orange juice at the hospital, I began to feel more secure about living a full life again. By morning I felt almost normal and, after breakfast, Al and I rented a car and drove back to Long Island.

I was so happy to be alive that I wanted to get right back in the lineup and play the next night at Nassau Coliseum; only this time I made sure I had salt pills in my locker and trainer Ron Waske had oxygen on the bench.

Another painful part of a hockey player's life is the same as it is for a file clerk, a psychiatrist, or a schoolboy; and that is the trip to the dentist. It kills me just to think about going to have my teeth fixed. In fact, I'd much rather break a leg than have to go to the dentist, especially if he's going to give me the needle.

I've heard other hockey players talk the same way. They're a bundle of courage on the ice and they don't blink an eyelash when the doctor sews them up for a dozen stitches. But for some reason the dentist and his drill send chills up and down the spine of a stickhandler.

My personal theory is that the smell of the dentist's office tends to frighten the average person; it's like a hospital smell multiplied by ten and then underlined by the fearsome drill apparatus.

To cope with my obsessive fear of dentists and my greatest fear of all, losing a tooth—I have *never* lost a tooth—I wear a special mouth guard that our dentist, Dr. Jeffrey Smitten, designed for several of the Islanders. I have sworn by that mouth guard ever since the night we played the Philadelphia Flyers and I collided with Bill Barber.

At the moment of impact, Barber toppled over with his razor-sharp skate-blades pointing up. The back portion of the skate-blade, which is protected by a thick plastic covering, crashed against my mouth. Geez, I said more in fear than anger, I finally lost a couple.

I skated to the bench, my mouth feeling very much as if it were a series of nuts on an auto tire that had been well loosened in preparation for removing a flat. But the pain wasn't as bad as the time I had trying to remove the teeth protector from my mouth.

Barber's skate had hit the protector so hard it had actually caved it into my mouth, creating a suction so tight that getting it free was like opening up a hermetically sealed can with a defective can opener.

After several pulls, tugs, and pushes, I finally worked it free and discovered that a minor miracle had taken place. All my teeth were intact, even though the mouth guard was a wreck.

Most of us inured ourselves to pain early in our hockey careers; otherwise we wouldn't have reached the NHL. I have played with pain so often it has become second nature with me. My philosophy is directed at my psyche: Denis, if your machine can work, it will work, whether there's pain or not. The degree of pain is irrelevant as long as I can get the machine to work. Eddie Westfall played with a broken foot during the 1976 playoffs. The degree of pain didn't matter to him; Eddie was determined to play. It doesn't matter that you may have a broken finger that hurts like a bitch; if you can handle a stick and shoot the puck, you can play no matter how intense the pain—unless you happen to be a curiosity like Gilles Gratton.

Gratton had played goal for Oshawa in the OHA Junior A League when I was with Ottawa; later he played for Ottawa and Toronto of the WHA before coming to the NHL and St. Louis in 1975. They called him "Grattoony" because he was one of the looniest skaters ever to come down the pike, goaltenders or not. Once in the WHA he came out to a Toros' practice with nothing on his body but a pair of skates; he was hockey's first streaker! He played for Team Canada 1974 and posed nude in a sauna. The photo ran in almost every paper in Canada.

There were stories going around that, instead of listening to his coach, he listened to his astrologer. Guys tell me he believes that he has been reincarnated as a goaltender but had actually lived in 14th-century Spain; and he's serious about it. Gratton also happens to be a good goaltender when he isn't consulting the stars, and he looked like he might be an asset to the Blues in 1975–76 after they lured him away from the WHA.

But I remembered reports of Gratton in juniors: He was one of those players who refused to play with a minor injury. I had never seen Gratton's act until one night in December 1975 at Nassau Coliseum. Blues coach Garry Young had started Gratton against us and he seemed to be playing a competent game—no score in the first period—when Bobby Nystrom moved over the blue line on the right side and unloaded a harmless backhand shot. Gratton seemed to deflect it with his shoulder and then, the next thing I knew, he was on the ice, grimacing in pain.

The trainer rushed out and tried to rub Gratton's arm, but Gilles seemed determined to get off the ice. He skated to the bench and took himself off the ice. Old Eddie Johnston had to move in between the pipes as his replacement.

"That puck couldn't have hurt him," Nystrom said.

I told Bobby, "No wonder the Blues are having trouble."

Now that Johnston was in the net, Gratton left the bench altogether. Although I didn't see what happened, I heard that Young and Blues President Sid Salomon III gave Gratton a thorough going-over in the dressing room. They must have; Gilles never played another game for the Blues. St. Louis released him and, lo and behold, in March the Rangers, of all teams, signed him. When I heard that I said to myself, Perfect. I couldn't have asked for a better move.

By now the whole world is aware that the Soviet Army Team pulled the quit move of all time in 1976 when they walked off the ice in the midst of a game against the Philadelphia Flyers. Of course, some claim that it was strictly a strategic move—and maybe it was; guys on a pro hockey rink never stop looking for an edge, even if it means buttering up the opposition with a lot of verbal applesauce.

There are several NHL players who try to cultivate a pleasant talking relationship with the enemy. Guys like Bill Barber, Steve Shutt, and Phil Esposito butter up the opposition. They have a cutesy way of operating that appears very simple on the surface, a sort of Mister Nice Guy approach to the game that is actually meant to disarm tougher opponents.

Their weapon is plain talk, the kind you'd expect to hear strolling around a golf course—but not during a tough hockey game. I'll line up against Phil Esposito and he'll look up at me with his sloe eyes, his mouth turning to a grin, and he'll say, "How're ya doin', Denis? How was the trip?"

I know damn well that he's trying to get me to drop my guard so I'll lay off him a bit, letting him exploit that moment of unintended relaxation. He wants me to be thinking, Well, Phil is a nice guy, almost a friend even though he's a Ranger, so I won't hit him as hard as a Dave Schultz. Next thing I know, Esposito has skated right around me!

I didn't learn these things overnight; it took me about a season to make a "book" on the opposition. The process is similar to that in baseball. A pitcher may dazzle you with his fastball the first time around, but on the second or third meeting you may discover that he doesn't have anything else, and you learn to adjust to his weapon. In hockey, one of the factors you have to assess (for your own survival) is toughness. There are players who, on first impression, will make like Godzilla, King of the Monsters, but after a few "tests" they turn into *papier maché.*

Bob Gassoff of the St. Louis Blues marauded around the league in his rookie year like a bull in a china shop and those who did not have the book on Gassoff stayed out of his way. But inevitably there are players who can tell you whether he was a genuine toughie in juniors. (A player usually retains his character when he reaches the NHL.) My first memory of Gassoff on a rampage was at his home rink, the St. Louis Arena. He was running around, bopping our players like a boulder bouncing off trees as it careens down a mountain. I turned to Clark Gillies. "How do you stop a guy like that?" I asked.

"Watch this, Denis," said one of the biggest and strongest young players in the NHL.

Clark leaped over the boards. Right away the play went into the corner of the rink, Gassoff went to get it, and Gillies went right after him. But this time Clark completely ignored the puck and rammed Gassoff head-on. That was for starters; every time Gassoff touched the puck, Gillies ignored the rubber and bodied Gassoff in one way or another, punching him, slapping him, checking him, annoying him in every imaginable way.

Finally, the whistle blows and Gillies has Gassoff pinned against the boards. Clark pulls back, drops his huge leather gauntlets, and implicitly challenges Gassoff: C'mon, let's go!

This is hockey's High Noon. Does Gassoff go, or doesn't he?

For two seconds everybody on the ice stopped to see the dénouement. Gassoff turned, facing Gillies head-on. Their eyes met, then, without uttering a word, Gassoff hunched his shoulders forward, spread his gloves at both ends of his stick, and remained in a crouched position, his stick now resting on his knees. He was feigning fatigue, but everyone knew that the battle was won without a shot being fired.

A few minutes later Gillies skated back to our bench with a big, cocky grin on his face. I smiled back. "Clarkie, now I see what you mean."

Another time I did the same favor for Gillies. We were playing the Toronto Maple Leafs and one of their big defensemen, Bob Neely, was trying to intimidate some of our smaller men. Now, Neely comes in at six-feet-one, 210 pounds, which is a lot of muscle if it rams you the wrong way, and some of our guys were afraid of him.

But I knew Neely when he played against me for Peterborough of the OHA Junior A League, and I knew that he wasn't all that tough. "Look," I told the guys, "just go tell Neely that you're goin' to shove your stick down his throat, or you're goin' to kick his ass in. Just show him you're not afraid."

So here we are in Maple Leaf Gardens, Neely's home rink, and he's running around, showing off his toughness, when our little Garry Howatt takes a run at him. Then Neely turns and heads up to center ice, and I crash him to the ice. Next time he invaded our territory there was a pile-up in front of the net, everyone jumping on top of each other, getting in little shots, and Neely got it left and right.

In a bristling situation like this, Neely has an option: he can come up swinging; he can come up like a normal person, hoping the referee will call a penalty against our club; or he can pat *our* guys on the back.

Why in hell would a member of the opposition suddenly become palsy-walsy in the midst of a turbulent scene in which he had been one of the most belligerent performers?

The answer is simple enough: We had softened up Neely to such an extent that, by patting us on the back, he was symbolically raising the white flag of surrender. Neely was saying, I don't want any part of you anymore!

Some guys would do that all the time—pat us on the back—and I'd hate it. He was implicitly trying to say, If you don't hurt me, I won't hurt you. Or, even if you *do* hurt me, I'm still not going to hurt you!

There are, of course, guys who *can* hurt you without laying a hand on your person; they just lay their fingers on the typewriter. I'm talking about the hockey writing fraternity, the men who can do more to give a player pain than any "policeman" on the opposition.

I remember, when I was playing junior hockey in Ottawa, how I'd read every piece of hockey literature available, especially when it was about guys against whom I had played and who now were in the NHL. There was one article that really stung, written by Stan Fischler in *Action Sports Hockey* magazine, in which Stan was very harsh on Billy Harris, who then was an Islanders' rookie.

The article stuck in my craw because I knew Billy (having played against him), liked him, and realized that one day, soon, we might be teammates on the Islanders. I felt that Stan was unfairly tough on Billy, who was only a rookie playing on what was then the worst team in hockey history. Reading the piece made me realize how vulnerable an athlete can be, especially a young player as sensitive about his game as Harris.

When I reached the NHL, I made a point of keeping an open mind about the media. I wanted to gain their respect, yet I knew that, in time, there would be writers for whom I would have respect and others whom I would loathe. The ones I came to dislike were those who took unfair advantage of a player in one way or another, especially when it came to language difficulties. English-speaking writers invariably have no command of French, yet they expect French-speaking players to have a thorough working knowledge of English during interviews.

I get furious when I find English-speaking writers burning our Jude Drouin (accidentally, no doubt) because Drouin doesn't express himself as well in English as he does in French. What Jude says frequently appears in print just the opposite of what he meant to say. The reporters are not patient enough with the individual players. It's a sort of hit-and-run deal; if Drouin says a few words, instead of probing to find out precisely what he means, the writers run on to the next guy.

What irks me about the press is their endless quest for controversy where none obviously exists. On our club, newsmen seemed determined to build up a "rivalry" between our two goalies, Chico Resch, an extrovert who is extremely popular with the fans, and Billy Smith, who is more withdrawn and once expressed a desire to play more games on the road than at home because of the lack of affection he felt at Nassau Coliseum. For a time in 1975, reporters kept pressuring Smitty to say something unpleasant about Chico. What the newsmen didn't seem to understand—or chose not to believe—was that these two goalies have a uniquely positive relationship despite the fact that they both want to play as many games as possible.

Some writers will throw questions to try to get responses that will eventually incriminate the player. They'll confront the player when he's upset, pump him with questions aimed at a particular "angle" (even if there is no "angle" there at all), and work over the player until he falls victim to the trap. That's the kind of reporter with whom a player should not talk unless he absolutely can't avoid the interview. On the other hand, a guy like Sid Payne of *The Long Island Press,* one of the most knowledgeable hockey writers, will never stab you in the back in print. He is utterly straightforward and will put the question directly to me: "Denis," Payne will say, "you haven't been playing well; can we discuss it?"

That's fine with me. I'm a professional athlete and if I'm not playing well, I have an obligation to discuss the matter with the media—but the media has an obligation to treat me fairly. I hate those writers who come into the dressing room and hide in the background while others ask me questions. It's very important to me to see the reporter, eye-to-eye, and see him write my words on paper.

So, in time, I developed my "book" on writers. The best are veterans Red Fisher of *The Montreal Star,* Bob Verdi of *The Chicago Tribune,* and a kid on *Newsday* named Pat Calabria. I can sit down with Calabria and feel at ease, without feeling as if I'm being exploited.

On the other hand, some reporters will invite me to play tennis and, on the surface, it will appear as if we're having a friendly day on the courts. But that's not the motive. When we're through playing, he'll start asking hockey questions directed toward some aspect of the Islanders. I can do without that.

Even more disturbing is the manner in which the press zeroes in on the negative rather than the positive side of a team's—or an individual's—play. In 1975–76, I made the First All-Star Team and won the Norris Trophy as the NHL's best defenseman. Yet to read some of the stories during the season, you'd think I was having a bummer of a year. As Jean Beliveau once told me, "The press always seems to expect more than you can accomplish."

There was a night in March 1976 when we defeated the California Seals, 2–1, at Nassau Coliseum. The next day Jim O'Brien of *The New York Post* described my game as "a dreadful performance."

It seemed that all the good that had been accomplished in the five previous months was wiped out with one mediocre effort *even though I helped the club win the game.* Thanks to reports like that, I found that I was getting fewer cheers than I might ordinarily have received—mostly because of the media's fascination for the negative.

Not long after O'Brien's "dreadful" performance piece, *The New York Times* ran a feature with the headline, NO CHEERS FOR POTVIN.

The last thing I wanted was to be naive about the position of the press and my own image. I've never been a crowd favorite wherever I've played. The reason is obvious: I'm a top player and the people take me for granted. I'm expected to do no wrong, so when I do make a mistake O'Brien says it was a "dreadful" performance. Maybe I should be honored.

Style has also had a lot to do with the media's reaction to professional athletes. They loved Bobby Orr—even though Orr rarely said a word to the press in ten years—because of his dazzling skating ability. But could he accomplish as much as I can with simpler, more team-oriented maneuvers? I'll put a guy in on the power play with a pass; he'll score the goal, so it doesn't reflect as brightly on me. Long afterward, people may realize that the puck went through two opponents as I laid it right on my teammate's stick.

While the press is annoying in a distant way, referees are among the most immediately grating aspects of playing pro hockey. For some reason some referees have gotten the mistaken impression that fans come to see *them* rather than the players. As a result, they have hurt the game and the players because of their power hunger. The people pay to see a hockey game, not a damn referee bouncing around trying to be a showman.

We're usually helpless to do anything about the officiating. You *can* talk to a good referee such as Andy Van Hellemond. But if a poor referee calls a bum game and you try to question him, he'll give you a ten-minute misconduct penalty just for *looking* at him.

Only once since I've been playing pro hockey have I seen a team get back at an official. We were the team; Dave Newell was the official. It happened at Nassau Coliseum late in the 1975–76 season. We were playing the Minnesota North Stars, a bad hockey club that was doing everything right against us that night. In the second period we seemed to be playing with four skaters instead of five, thanks to Newell's calls.

It took almost the entire game, but we finally got even with the referee. We were down to the last minute of the game, killing a penalty with one man short. It's a situation in hockey where you can shoot the puck down the ice without being called for "icing" the puck. By this time we were all so furious with Newell's officiating that any one of the 18 guys would have loved to take a shot at him.

As luck would have it, Jude Drouin happened to intercept the puck in the right corner, deep in the Islanders' zone. And standing temptingly alongside the boards at the other side of the rink was referee Newell. Drouin looked up, wound up an "icing" shot, and blasted it straight around the boards. The puck hit the ref and then landed at his skates. By now, Jude was moving behind the net in the direction of the puck. With the puck at Newell's skates, Drouin swung all right, this time knocking the skates right out from under Newell and sending the official down unceremoniously on his *derrière!* Drouin had done all this, of course, strictly according to the book. After all, the referee was right in the path of the puck and, then, of Drouin.

Newell whistled Drouin off the ice with a ten-minute misconduct and then tagged on a game misconduct penalty, which meant that NHL President Clarence Campbell would have to conduct a hearing on the matter. Jude could easily wind up with a suspension for allegedly trying to harm a referee.

For several days we held our collective breath, wondering whether Drouin would get the severe penalty that some people feared he would. The Islanders' argument was that the two blows suffered by Newell were coincidental accidents, that the referee happened to be in the wrong place at the wrong time. Campbell finally ruled that way, and Jude escaped without any further penalty.

# 19

## CRYING OUT OF HAPPINESS

Happiness for Armand Potvin was not a Cadillac, a motorboat, or a swimming pool in the backyard. All my father has ever wanted out of life, once it was evident that he would be physically unable to play major league hockey, was to have one of his sons make it to the bigs.

When Jean signed with the Los Angeles Kings, Armand Potvin was a happy man. When I put my signature on a New York Islanders' contract, it was euphoria multiplied by two for Dad. If it were possible to have made him any happier, Jean and I accomplished that on January 22, 1976, at Nassau Coliseum.

Our opponents were the Detroit Red Wings, a lowly club we should have handled with ease. But, as often happens, we got careless early in the game, and at 4:36 Dennis Polonich fired the puck past Billy Smith in our net. We looked lost until late in the period when the Red Wings got a penalty and Al Arbour sent out our power play.

There was a time when our power play was the laughing stock of the league. Guys like Brad Park, Derek Sanderson, and Pete Stemkowski of the Rangers used to needle our hides when our club was young until we hated them with a passion. We were determined to build our power play until it was the best in the NHL. By the middle of the 1975–76 season we had done the impossible; not only did we have the best penalty-killers in Lorne Henning and Eddie Westfall, but our power play had scored even more goals than that of the Montreal Canadiens' or the then Stanley Cup-champion Philadelphia Flyers.

Some believe that I played a large part in that transformation. "Denis Potvin runs the best power play in the league," said Rod Gilbert of the Rangers. "You need somebody to direct traffic and he's the guy."

But it takes more than one man to make a power play. I was working with three splendid forwards: Bryan Trottier at center, Clark

Gillies on left wing, and Billy Harris on the right. I played the "point" along with brother Jean.

From an impotent laughing stock ("It was a joke," Billy Harris told me), our power play turned into the most awesome scoring threat in the league ("It's no longer a joke," added Harris). Captain Westfall, who was there in the doldrum days, had the best explanation:

"Balance and movement are the ingredients that make ours the best," said Eddie. "You need good balance among the guys involved. They must be good puck handlers and shooters. In moving the puck they have to ease the penalty-killers, get them out of position, and get them to make a mistake that will free a man for a shot."

A power play in hockey uses elements of both football and basketball. Gillies, who stands six-feet-three and weighs 220 pounds, is like a blocking back running interference for Harris.

Gillies has the size and he creates disturbances in the slot. Trottier is the stickhandler and corner worker. Harris is the shooter with good speed. Jean is the backstop with an excellent shot, and I like to move up from the point whenever possible, always considering a cross-ice pass to Jean. Or, as Phil Esposito once told *Newsday,* "Denis controls it, but he has a lot of help."

That night in January we were getting so much help from one another that Detroit goalie Jimmy Rutherford, who was watching the game from the sidelines, later said, "I'd rather face a penalty shot than that Islanders power play. They can really wear you down."

We wore them down with Barry Salovaara in the penalty box, but we couldn't score. Salovaara had been out of the box only ten seconds when Jean and Bobby Nystrom combined on passes to put the puck in front of the Detroit net, where I lifted it over goalie Peter McDuffe. Before the period ended, J. P. Parise had put us ahead. But the fun for the Potvins had just begun.

At 4:41 of the second period I helped set up Jean for his first goal of the game, on the power play. At 18:06 he got his second one. At 18:27 the Wings got another penalty, so the coach sent Jean and me out on the points again. This time Jude Drouin and I set up Jean, and at 18:51 of the second period he had scored the "hat trick," three goals in one game. Jean skated over to me, bubbling with joy. "Denis," he said, "I damn near swallowed my mouthpiece!"

Armand and Lucille Potvin were at home in Ottawa, where they were listening to the game on two radios, one tuned to the Islanders' station, WMCA, the other to WJR in Detroit. They didn't want to miss anything.

At 1:18 of the third period I gave them a little more to cheer about when I scored my second goal of the game and the fifth for the Potvin family. Now the sellout crowd of 14,865 began chanting for me to get a "hat trick," too.

I wanted that third goal, but I didn't want to steal my brother's thunder. As the third period progressed and the Red Wings disintegrated, I had a few better-than-average scoring chances, but I missed all of them. In retrospect, I'm glad I did. I wanted very much for Jean to get some attention.

Ever since my signing with the Islanders, I had gotten the ink and Jean had gotten the shadows. It was an inevitable situation, I suppose, but it was one I couldn't relish because of my love for Jean and my admiration of him as an artist and a professional. What made the night so ironic was that after we had beaten the Wings, 8–1, as we savored the win in the dressing room later on, Jean kept talking about *me*.

"It's a dream come true for us to play on the same team," said Jean. "You know, I can still remember the day he was drafted by the Islanders. When they made the announcement, I couldn't hold back the tears. I was Denis' biggest fan then, and I'm his biggest fan now."

Perhaps it sounded corny, but I know Jean meant every word of it, and I feel the same way about him. Every time we skated out on the ice together the feeling was too unreal to be believed. Which is the way I felt on March 29, 1976.

After the game in which Jean and I combined for five goals, I had a season-long total of 20, with 35 games remaining on the schedule. Reporters began speculating on my chances of reaching the 30-goal plateau.

"Do you know of any other NHL defenseman who scored 30?" one of the reporters asked me.

"Only one," I said with as much intensity as I could develop, "Bobby Orr!"

I desperately wanted to reach Orr's 30-goal level. The Bruins' ace had been sidelined for much of the season, and here I was playing the best hockey of my life. Something tangible and unique, like a 30th goal, would underline my accomplishments.

My chances of hitting number 30 were not very good on the night of March 29. Our opponents were the Philadelphia Flyers, one of the best defensive teams in the NHL, and the team that had beaten us out of first place in the Lester Patrick Division the year before.

A lot of people had figured the Flyers for phony champions in 1973–74 on the ground that they had taken the overconfident Bruins by surprise in the Stanley Cup finals and had then been lucky in getting past the Rangers in the seven-game semi-finals. Having gone against them in hand-to-hand combat, I knew differently. They had a remarkable club and one of the most inspiring leaders anywhere in their captain Bobby Clarke.

When the Flyers beat us and Buffalo to win the Cup in 1975, nobody called them phony champs anymore. But a season later their ace goalie, Bernie Parent, pulled up lame, and it became apparent that they would have to go the entire 1975–76 season using a second-stringer named Wayne Stephenson. That's why we thought we had a shot at first place in the Patrick Division that season. But as the new year began, the Flyers refused to fold, and when they came to Nassau at the end of March, they had first place all sewed up.

This stung us to the core; we genuinely felt that we had arrived in 1975–76, that our little "miracle" of Nassau County was no more a fluke than the Flyers' success. And after two years of my being the Islanders' "name" player, critics had come to expect that I would supply the same kind of leadership that Clarke had for Philly. I knew I wasn't the same rah-rah personality that Clarke was, that my leadership was more by example than by verbosity. I could only sit down next to a guy on the bench and try to explain to him what I thought he should do.

Time and again I felt the urge to be more flamboyant, to play the Bobby Orr role. But I knew deep down that that was *not* what I really wanted—or what was good for Denis Potvin. I knew I'd rather draw two guys in and pass instead of trying to rush. Or I'll decide not to rush if my wings aren't back to cover for me. But I'll rush if they send only one man in to cover for me, and I'll have a better than even chance to beat him. I knew I had made the right decision when I picked up *The Montreal Gazette* and read Tim Burke's column about me: "When Numero Uno places the system ahead of himself, you have a helluva ball club."

The Flyers do not like numero unos. They like to cut them down to size with their usual assortment of checks, double checks, and an occasional spear or elbow. On the night of March 29 I took the ice more determined than ever to play my best against the best, to show that in my own more subtle way I can be to the Islanders what a Bobby Clarke is to the Flyers.

"Okay," said the coach as we headed out on the rubber mat toward the ice, "let's make things happen!"

It took exactly three-and-a-half minutes for us to fulfill the request. I spotted our rookie center Bryan Trottier busting free and shot the kind of pass that I knew he could handle as he catapulted himself into scoring position. The kid made things a lot easier for all of us, and especially for me, because the other teams have concentrated more on Bryan. They have to; he's tough and he's got those powerful legs you need for hockey speed. With the puck on his stick, it was only a matter of seconds before he had shot it past Stephenson. We were ahead, 1–0. Within four minutes André St. Laurent made it 2–0, then I fed Garry Howatt and we had the champs down, 0–3, before the first period was half over. The crowd of 14,865 was needling the Flyers with a chorus of *God Bless America*.

Two assists had only whet my appetite and I was thirsting for a goal. My next goal would be my 30th. How could I get it without being greedy, without sacrificing my sense of team for the satisfaction of my ego?

Fortunately, we held the Flyers scoreless for a period and a half, and we still led, 3–0. At 10:25 of the second period Flyers defenseman Tom Bladon was whistled off for two minutes. Arbour sent me over the boards to orchestrate the power play. This is your chance, Denis, I muttered. Don't go crazy; let it happen in its own way, if it's goin' to happen.

For more than a minute of the power play, it looked like nothing was going to happen. Then the old boys, Eddie Westfall, J. P. Parise, and Jude Drouin came on, replacing the Kid Line. About 20 seconds before Bladon was due to return to the ice, Westfall and Parise began teasing the Flyers' defense with passes when the puck came back to me at the point.

I moved about ten feet toward Stephenson and cranked up the shot. It was hard, true, and, although one never knows for sure until the red light flashes, I sensed that this could be the big one. At 12:10 the light went on.

People *say* that men should never be ashamed to cry in public if they have good reason, but this is not an easy thing to *do;* you always want to give the impression of being masculine. This time I couldn't restrain myself.

When I saw the fans clapping and then begin rising from their seats to give me a standing ovation, I remembered the guy who had told me once why fans don't take to me as easily as they do to more charismatic players. "You're maddening," the guy said, "because everything on the ice looks so easy for you." What he didn't know was that I die out there a lot of the time.

This time the fans seemed to realize what had gone into my 30 goals and were rewarding me for it. The ovation went on and on and I knew I was crying. What bothered me was the television and newspaper cameras trained on me; I desperately wanted to hide my head from them.

My teammates, on the other hand, took the 30th goal as if they had expected it to happen. Nobody said anything to me on the ice. It was discouraging because I wanted very much to be congratulated by my buddies. Anyone, even a First All-Star, needs a confidence-builder from time to time. You need to know your buddies believe you're playing well.

The cacophony of the crowd that night didn't stop after just a few seconds; it went on and on until the entire audience was on its feet. It was too much. I skated to the bench, fell to the wooden plank, and bawled—as quietly as I could before 14,865 friends. Somehow I managed to keep a lot of the tears inside, but Jean leaned over and handed me a towel. I was crying out of happiness. Denis Potvin, who prides himself on his supreme sense of control, could no longer control himself.

I didn't care. I was crying for Lucille and Armand and Jean and for the completion of Denis' dream. If I needed any confirmation, it was there in black and white. Jim Proudfoot, sports editor of *The Toronto Star* and one of the most respected hockey critics in the world, put it precisely the way I had hoped someone would: POTVIN BECOMES NUMBER ONE DEFENSEMAN RIGHT ON SCHEDULE.

All of a sudden the years of inner fury at being called "the next Bobby Orr" seemed worthwhile.

# EPILOGUE

By June 1976, when I finally hung my shingle—Denis Potvin, Ltd.—on the door of People & Properties at 919 Third Avenue, I realized that in spirit if not in fact I was now more American than Canadian. I was a hockey player, I was in business, and Debbie and I had taken an apartment on the East Side of Manhattan overlooking the East River.

What I had done was to take the bull by the horns in a manner totally uncharacteristic of the French-Canadian Denis from Ottawa. Instead of being orchestrated by others, *I* was doing the conducting for the Potvin Concerto in B (for Bucks) Sharp.

Remember the distinction. I had never really chosen hockey as a profession; it was there and I was talented. I played the game and loved it—and still do. Everything fell into place for me in hockey with such ease that I never had to initiate anything on my own.

I came to New York not because *I* made the choice but because I had been drafted in the NHL market. I was taken by somebody and brought to New York just as I had been taken by somebody and entered in junior hockey. But being in New York meant that doors suddenly began opening on vistas that I never dreamed existed. As the doors opened, I peeked through them and liked what I saw. Then I started taking those first few steps alone; nobody was pushing me and it was a different, a wonderful feeling.

I looked into the marketing field, thanks to Tony Andrea and Edd Griles, who steered me in that direction, and I liked the feel of the business. In three years I felt I had a pretty good idea of what it was all about, and I decided that marketing would be my *other* vocation. When I feel it's time to retire from hockey, I'll be able to move into People & Properties.

One might wonder just how a fellow whose education reached only the 12th grade of high school could compete with the wizards of

Madison Avenue. The answer is that I've developed myself in other ways—in street knowledge, you might say. Reading has really improved my vocabulary (I went through a period where I'd read almost anything) and I'm a voracious crossword puzzle addict.

A week after I returned to New York from the awards ceremony in Montreal I picked up the June 1976 issue of *Sport* magazine.

I read the title of the article on page 74, "The Hockey Player Who Turned Down The Montreal Canadiens."

Then I did a double take. The author was none other than Earl McRae, the same fellow who had written the first major piece about me for *The Canadian* when I was still with the Ottawa 67s.

Once again, McRae was writing about a top-rated junior. His name was Robin Sadler. He was 20 years old and had been one of the finest junior hockey players in the world, playing defense for the Edmonton Oil Kings. He was strong, tall, and superbly gifted—but he hated hockey!

It was unbelievable.

The Canadiens had given him a contract worth $250,000 over three years, plus an $80,000 bonus. In September 1975, when I was launching my most glorious season with the Islanders, Sadler went to the Canadiens' training camp, supposedly fulfilling every Canadian boy's dream.

Less than two weeks later Robin Sadler walked away from the hockey wars. He tore up his quarter-of-a-million-dollar contract, gave back the bonus money (which he could have kept), and returned to the mountains of British Columbia to find a job that was, as he put it, "fun." He wound up driving a delivery truck for a drug store. Instead of earning $1,600 a week, he was taking in $160. Instead of driving a Mercedes, Sadler was piloting a beat-up 1962 Chevy.

He said he didn't mind it a bit, that he questioned hockey's demands when he first came up to Junior A. "I just didn't like it," he said. "All those stupid rules like curfews and things. They treat you like a kid, always checking to see if you're in bed. They practiced three times a day and nobody smiled, nobody laughed. Everybody was uptight, fighting for jobs.

"Guys were even fighting each other in practice. It was just ridiculous. To me, hockey was always a game, that's all, something I played to enjoy, you know, a lot of fun. But these people treated it like some kind of business."

It seemed strange to me that Sadler, even at age 18, would interpret the machinations of organized junior hockey as anything other than a business. He didn't quit, though; he played junior hockey again in Vancouver, and then in Edmonton. Toward the end of his last junior season he was beaten up during a game and apparently wasn't the same player after that, although Sadler claimed the fight itself had had nothing to do with his decision. In fact, he got Al Eagleson to represent him, and he signed that big, fat NHL contract.

"The press, the people, everybody was making a big fuss over me," Sadler explained, "telling me I'm going to be a big star; everybody's pushing me to go."

So Robin Sadler went—and returned home.

His story saddened me in a way. This was a young man with exceptional potential who obviously did not care to dedicate himself to the game.

Apparently he was not ready to accept the fact that life—whether it be the hockey life, life behind a desk, or the life down in a coal mine—requires the expenditure of sweat and maybe a little blood. He may have been afraid to make that commitment.

In a way I could sympathize with him. Nobody likes to be regimented, least of all me. Curfews are in a way kid stuff. But this is part of the code and, like it or not, it must be observed. Discipline must be learned; it's all part of growing up.

I thought of Sadler as I walked to my office at 919 Third Avenue. At 23, I was a success on ice and a success in business, but only because I was willing to pay the price.

If I'm really lucky, I'll take one more step in the not too distant future and sip champagne from the Stanley Cup, along with Debbie, Armand, Lucille, and Jean Potvin.

# INDEX